THE
MBA RUN

THE MBA RUN

Mansie Dewan

STERLING PAPERBACKS
An imprint of
Sterling Publishers (P) Ltd.
Regd. Office: A-59, Okhla Industrial Area, Phase-II,
New Delhi-110020. CIN: U22110PB1964PTC002569
Tel: 26387070, 26386209; Fax: 91-11-26383788
E-mail: mail@sterlingpublishers.com
www.sterlingpublishers.com

The MBA Run
© 2015, Mansie Dewan
ISBN 978 81 207 9885 4

All rights are reserved.
No part of this publication may be reproduced, stored in a retrieval system or transmitted, in any form or by any means, mechanical, photocopying, recording or otherwise, without prior written permission of the publisher.

Printed in India

Printed and Published by Sterling Publishers Pvt. Ltd., New Delhi-110 020.

Foreword

The detailed account of an MBA aspirant's journey (unedited). A must read! Even if you skip some sections of the book, don't skip this.

I have recently been accepted to one of the schools of my choice, and to cut the long story short, I feel that I have warped through the last year. Such has been the journey till date that for me MBA translates to Most Brain-racking Adventure—and I am yet to join the program. But, weirdly enough, it has already been a rewarding adventure.

The views expressed here are coming from someone just like you (not from an MBA guru), and so they have to be taken with a pinch of salt.

First of all, MBA is not the end of this world. You do not *have* to be one to be successful, happy or feel respected. So, if you are hell-bent on getting an MBA, you should be able to convince yourself of the reason why it is so. A good way to start doing it is to really introspect about what you love about your current job. Once you can figure that out you can unearth the strengths you use most of the time. Next, think about what your ideal job could be and see how that differs from your current job. If the differences lie in maximizing or building on your current strengths, you *may not* need an MBA to start doing that. However, if you can identify elements missing in your skill set, you may need to develop new ones. An MBA can certainly help in that regard. Do an MBA if, and only if, what an MBA gives you and what you are looking for are a perfect match. Else, it's a futile effort of matching a triangle with a square.

Once you are convinced that an MBA is the way to go, the first hurdle is the GMAT. I have heard people spending enormous amount of time, not on the exam per se, but on a ridiculously high number of preparatory materials. The flow of action should be — get the basics right, practise until satisfied, take a few mock exams to see if you are where you want to be, and minor tweaks thereon. This does not necessarily mean poring over millions of pages of practice material. Plan your preparation wisely. The MBA journey begins sooner than you think.

The actual task begins once you have a GMAT score in your hands. The first thing you should understand is that GMAT is only one part of an enormous data-set that any school evaluates. So there is no need to break your head over it. It should just act as a marker as to where you stand and which colleges you may apply to. The only consideration here should be that you should not apply to a college where the GMAT score will become an eliminating factor. As long as that is taken care of, you should be fine.

So now that you have a GMAT score and you know a bunch of colleges you can or may apply to, the most difficult part begins.

Read as much as possible about the colleges you are targeting. The sheer amount of information available through their websites is staggering and can get easily overlooked. Once you religiously go through it, you will start zeroing in on the colleges that really attract you. The initial 20 or so colleges will quickly become 10. At this stage it is important to understand how each college is different from any other. Keeping a list of attributes or things you like about a college will help in making decisions. The subtle differences between the colleges are the basics on which you will start building your resumes, essays and interview responses. Colleges love to know that the candidate has done his or her research.

A parallel activity will be honest and prolonged introspection. This takes a lot of time and, I mean — a lot of time. To answer simple questions like "Why MBA?", "Why a particular college?" etc., you will end up spending days ,if not weeks. Do not rush through, as this is critical to your success. Only when you are aware of the colleges' slightest differences, unique strengths and your own purpose, can you relate to each college meaningfully, and that attachment gets highlighted all through the application.

A few things to take care of at this stage:
- DO NOT use the same resume or essay replies for all colleges. Each college is unique and so should be your responses. Try and see which of your qualities or accomplishments align to the values and mission of a particualr college and frame your responses accordingly.

- Avoid redundancy — DO NOT repeat the same stories across resume, essays, etc., unnecessarily. Try and give a fuller picture by sharing multiple experiences. Make it interesting for people who are going to read them. Do put in considerable effort on the resume — the first material they will see. The first impression *is* a make or break for all.

- Get your written stuff reviewed by a few people who can give ruthless, unbiased feedback. Small failures in front of them will translate into success in front of the admissions committee. In this regard, seeking help from a professional consultant may be of help as he or she has gone through this cycle many times in the past, and so comes equipped with invaluable insights.

Once you have gone through the above stages, the application is complete. Hopefully, after a brief wait you will bag a number of interview calls. That means the colleges will be happy to have you — you have passed the minimum requirements. Now, the only catastrophe that may happen is you messing up your own opportunities — an admit offer is yours to lose at this stage. Be calm and confident, as in any interview, and continue building on your college research and you should sail through.

A few things to take care of at this stage:
- Know your resume better than you know your own name. A resume is the foundation of all interviews, and so understand what you are trying to convey—prepare anecdotes and stories to corroborate and substantiate each point.
- Know the college and its MBA program better than "them". Your best friend here? Google.
- Connect with current students and alumni to get their perspectives. Not all experiences have been captured digitally. A phone call can do wonders.
- Keep your responses concise and to the point, however. Do not be robotic. Engage in a conversation as you would with a friend. The interviewers are giving you time to let yourself into the college. They are friendly.
- Know your interviewer before he or she knows you. This may not always be possible. But whenever it is, a little research can help you frame relevant questions to ask—it makes the interviewer happy.
- Do not panic. No matter what. A question has stumped you? Relax. The interviewer is not running away. Breathe, take your time and your brain will do the rest.
- The interviewer wants to know you. And you know yourself the best in the whole world. So you will always have the advantage. Be confident.

That's all the advice I can muster at this moment. I hope it makes sense and helps you. Lastly, you managed to read all of the above. Ah! You have what it takes to crack the offer—*patience*. You are all set.

At this point it should be abundantly clear that the most immersive, enriching and also confusing phase of the entire process is the phase of giving words to your thoughts—be it articulating your school choices, building the resume, perfecting your essays, or preparing for the interview. Just for an example, see if you can write down 5 of your strengths and weaknesses without thinking twice.

Foreword

Feel the crunch, eh!

Do not worry as this in only natural. What can be helpful, however, is having a guide who can help you shape your thoughts by channelling them in the right direction. In this regard, I can say Mansie madam and her team at MDC have helped me in spades. In retrospect, my decision to seek her advice was the best one I made last year. She not only maintained a "crystal clear feedback" approach from day 1, but also encouraged me to develop my own ideas in a way that they reflected my own work. That was a serious boost to my confidence and, I know, it has helped me over and over again. Also, she has always been very approachable and has always squeezed time out of her busy schedule to address any questions or doubts I had. In that regard, I believe that if I worked on my application for 24 hours a day, she did that for 48.

At this point all I can say to her is, "Thank You", but I believe that phrase falls short of doing its job.

ARINDAM DAS, 2015 *admit, UNC Kenan Flagler with USD 86K scholarship and UCLA Anderson with USD 40k scholarship.*

Acknowledgements

The MBA Run could not have been possible without the wealth of inspiration I have gained from my own clients over the years. To all of you who have endorsed me for this new book here and everyone else I have worked with over the years—I learn as much from you as you do from me. Thank you for allowing me the privilege of working with you and helping you refine your life strategies and applications! You inspire me and I am proud to have each one of you in my life. PagalGuy.com has provided me the platform to interact with thousands of aspirants, which has helped me phenomenally in building my own knowledge base for the book. For that, a special shout out to Allwin Agnel and his entire team!

A very special thanks to all the admissions committee members who agreed to participate in this project. I thank you for generously providing your time and insights to help MBA aspirants make better choices.

Thank you to Amit Kumar at Ezee Prep for helping with GMAT preparatory material and a special shout out to my friend, Kinjal Das, for double checking that everything's okay there.

For the book designing, formatting and layout, I must thank the very talented team at Sterling Publishers, who went out of their way to help and accommodate all my requests. My deepest gratitude goes out to Mr. S.K Ghai, without whose constant guidance and support, I wouldn't be where I am today. Sir, thank you from the bottom of my heart for making my dream of becoming a published author come true, the second time around.

Finally, I dedicate this book to you, dear reader. I hope you will draw useful insights from this book and use them to live your MBA dream.

I would love to hear from you with your feedback about this book. Write to me at mansie@mansiedewan.com.

Contents

Foreword — v

Acknowledgements — x

Introduction — 1

Testimonials — 3

1. **Strategies to get you started** — 17
   - Choosing your fit schools
   - Should you rely solely on rankings?
   - What you should really do
   - Features of your profile to help you decide on your target schools

2. **Preparing for the GMAT** — 23
   - What it entails
   - Understanding the scoring
   - Preparation
   - What study material do you need?
   - Course completion plan
   - Interview with the GMAC

3. **Working on the resume** — 33
   - Strategies for creating a strong MBA application resume.
   - A few common errors to avoid
   - Sample resumes

4. **Profiling, strategizing and building your essays**   **45**
   - The importance of work experience
   - Quality vs Quantity
   - Personal Attributes
   - How to craft impactful essays
   - Use the STAR approach
   - Specific pointers

5. **Interviews with admissions committees**   **51**
   - HEC Paris
   - ESADE Business School, Spain
   - HKUST
   - Georgetown McDonough
   - University of Rochester, Simon Business School
   - IE Business School, Spain
   - MISB Bocconi, Mumbai

6. **Sample essays**   **72**
   - Goals
   - Diversity and Contribution
   - Tell us about yourself
   - Achievements
   - Challenges
   - Strengths and Weaknesses
   - Leadership and Team Skills

INTRODUCTION

In today's day and age, the MBA is the most sought after degree. A strong foundation in business management, fortified by specialized career tracks and access to globally strong alumni networks, almost always ensure a fantastic return on investment. You've invested in this book; so an MBA is on your mind and you want to know more about how to get one! Let me show you how.

There is a common pattern among the people who get admitted to their desired business schools. They are successful in identifying which programs meet their needs and then marketing their candidatures effectively. They deserve special applause because most top ranked business schools receive enough applications from well qualified candidates, each of who meets the eligibility criteria (academics, GMAT, reports, resume, bullet points of responsibilities and achievements) perfectly. The schools are in a position to be extremely selective and, as a general rule, will shortlist only those candidates who will distinguish themselves and have a variety of experiences that will add significant value to their MBA classroom.

The admitted candidate is one who will put together an application which is perfect from each vantage point. They will demonstrate that special something extra, the special zing that indicates a rock solid potential for future success and contribution to the school. In the MBA application process, there are some parameters which remain fixed, such as GMAT and academic scores and the number of years of experience. Then there are the application essays that allow the admissions teams to look beyond the plain and simple data and know the person behind them, to get a sense of who the person is, what drives them, their value systems and view their experiences from their own perspective.

Constructing impactful essays is the most important aspect of the business school admissions process. The essays are perhaps the only component that YOU, as the candidate, can control. Through the sample essays here, I want to show you how applicants in the past have used their own unique stories to compel the admissions committee to want to know more about them, an important next step towards that admit. (All of these helped the aspirants get admitted too!) I've also requested a couple of my clients to share their own meaningful experiences in their own unique way, to empower YOU, the MBA aspirant, to a position of strength so as to approach this process in the most systematic way and multiply your chances of acceptance. Please use this book to learn how to tell YOUR unique stories in YOUR unique way.

Remember, Aspirants, the schools do not want to see applicants who sound like other applicants they've reviewed in the past, with similar stories to share! Be original—introspect, map your life, charter your trajectory and identify your uniqueness before you get down to making that application. Go, carve yourself a winning strategy and crack it!

TESTIMONIALS

Getting an admit from a reputed MBA program is a long process—starting from the GMAT preparation, to getting that admit mail.

I, initially, had difficulties in all these phases of the journey. Fortunately, I came across an article written by Mansie in *The Hindu* regarding MBA education. I decided to work along with her to make my dream come true. I was really happy with the way we started our work, first understanding myself—where exactly I was and where I wanted to be. This helped me get clarity on my goals and expectations from MBA programs.

To all the future aspirants, I would suggest to start the applications very early. Doing so will help you to get all the applications/recommendations well within the deadlines and, most importantly, you will get peace of mind. Mansie, as an accomplished professional in this field, helped me in this long process and helped me in achieving admits from 3 top B-Schools—Tepper, Georgetown and Texas Mays, with good scholarships. I'm sure Mansie's new book will help many more MBA aspirants to achieve their dream in a realistic manner. I wish her the best!

Hareesh Ramachandran, 2015 *admit, Texas Mays, Tepper and Georgetown with varying scholarships*

*****

I purchased and read Mansie's first book immediately after I wrote my GMAT and got a 750. I had aspirations to get into a top B-School and did not want my GMAT advantage to get ruined by my poor writing skills! :) I read her book, loved it, and immediately had an introductory chat with her about my profile and how she could help me in the application process.

She did 5 applications for me (plus 2 pro-bono application reviews), including at least 2 versions of each essay (I can be a real PITA to work with sometimes), guided me through the recommendation letter process, and framed an excellent action oriented resume for me. All this is fairly standard, but what is not is the fact that she got me interview calls at LBS, Wharton, Kellogg, Kenan-Flagler, Oxford Said and ESADE. Once again, quite a few consultants could have done that, given my profile. What they could not have done, and what I believe Mansie is truly strong at, is the fact that she helped me through all the depressions and low-confidence moments that I had throughout the application process. She is not just a consultant, she is a great coach, and an even better friend. She has placed many people in top B-Schools and almost all of them maintain regular contact with her because she is just an excellent person to work with. If you want a successful MBA application process, I strongly recommend that you read her book. I will not recommend that you sign her on as your consultant, because if you read her book, you will do that automatically. I can add a lot of other praises for her here, but I am going to let her book talk for itself. Read it. Seriously!

Sayak Bhattacharyya, *UNC Kenan Flagler CO 2016, recipient of merit fellowship with 50% tuition fee waiver*

*****

Testimonials

Applying to a top B-School abroad is, indeed, challenging. Feeling lost in the journey, I approached Mansie and sought her guidance, which eventually led me to my target school with a hefty scholarship. She knows the process in and out and her field expertise offers respite in this abstruse process. Mansie's book helps an applicant strategize his or her journey right from the inception of the idea of pursuing an MBA. From GMAT preparation, to preparing a compelling applicant profile, to scoring scholarship at top schools, every facet is detailed in the book. Many applicants underestimate the importance of a life story in essays and miss out interview calls despite having great academics and GMAT scores. This book will help you develop the art of making a multi-pronged impact on the admissions committee to ensure success.

Sumeet Sinha, *2015 admit, 80% scholarship at Kelley, 60% at Emory, 100%+stipend at Scheller & Arizona Carey*

*****

I'd like to thank you for all your guidance that helped me secure admission to two of my top colleges with scholarships! The odds were against me as I only had a limited work experience, but by working with you on my application essays, I was able to make a strong case for my acceptance. Another area where I feel you helped immensely was with mock interviews. You practiced with me several times and prepared me well in advance to answer any expected questions I would face. Thank you for your encouragement and I would recommend you without hesitation to future MBA applicants!

Raveena Godbole, *2015 admit, USD 40k scholarship at Olin and USD 62k scholarship at Rice*

*****

Mansie has created an important resource for students aspiring to pursue an MBA from some of the top schools. This well written book provides coverage of a number of key topics such as strategies to prepare for GMAT/GRE; methods to write impactful essays. Mansie has also covered topics which will help the reader to analyze more about herself/himself that would not only help to create better MBA applications, but also to help focus one's strengths. The information and selection criteria of some of the best schools is another add-on to this book. If only I had read this book earlier, my MBA journey would have been much simpler. Cheers!

Ashwin Baliwada, 2015 *admit*, CEO, *Cheers Group*, Cambridge

*****

Mansie has been a terrific friend and before I could say what I wanted, she was already prepared with suggestions for my application. Her insights about the application cycle and perception of school admission committee are just remarkable. I actually thought that I will write my own essays and I approached Mansie towards the very fag end of the deadline. She, in spite of keeping her commitments, helped me out as if she had known me since ages. She knew exactly what is required to be presented in the essays. It did not matter how well I wrote my own essays; it was important to understand how the admissions committees would review them. An interview call was at stake.

Mansie has remarkable insights developed over years of successful stories with her clients. I will suggest that you get the GMAT out of the way as early as possible and start working with Mansie, as more the time, better will be the application.

Thanks Mansie for all the help.

Kinjal Das, 2015 *admit*, Tepper and NUS

*****

Mansie has summarized perfectly how one should approach the B-School applications to ensure maximum output. I, and many aspirants, have followed the same path and landed our desired schools. I congratulate Mansie for such a wonderful effort to converge everything in a book and expect a lot of aspirants to be benefited by it.

Vaibhav Sharma, 2015 *admit, Darden and UNC Kenan Flagler*

*****

In Mansie I found an emphatic and perseverant individual with great work ethic. Her commitment and honesty towards her work reflects in her body of work. Her contribution to my MBA journey has been immense. She understands her craft well and has great insights about the nuances of admission process. Her unbiased guidance and support throughout the process was instrumental in getting admits in colleges of my choice. She motivated me at each step to not lose hope and settle for anything less than I deserved. I would recommend her to all my friends and anyone who has little or no understanding of the admission process.

All the best with your book.

Let me know when it is out. I look forward to read it.

It has been a wonderful experience working with you.

Thanks for all your support. I would not have been in a situation to choose between these universities without your guidance.

Bhavdeep Badesha, 2015 *admit, USD 46k scholarship at USC Moore and USD 70k scholarship at John Hopkins Carey*

*****

Having given my GMAT and done reasonably well on it, I felt smug and thought that the rest of the process would pretty much be a breeze. I couldn't have been more wrong. Two months on, and I was in no better shape as I was perplexed as to what to do and where to start. I would imagine that a lot of people go through this crisis—if I can call it that. To get some sort of reprieve (ideas), I decided to call a few admissions consultants, but grew increasingly disillusioned as I found that the consultants who talked to me sounded very formal and "played on the fence" which never gave me an "aha" moment. Enter Mansie.

Upon the suggestion of a friend and former classmate, who also raved about her first book, I decided to set up a call with Mansie—a very easy and prompt process if you go to her website. I had almost an hour long conversation with Mansie and felt an instant "connection" and she said all the "right things" that I wanted to hear. There was no looking back from there—Mansie's direction-oriented, logical and engaging approach helped me cruise past four applications (INSEAD, LBS, Kellogg and Columbia), of which I converted the one I wanted the most. The best part was that we worked as equals and there was no "formality"—just the way I like it! In fact, we even caught up for a cup of coffee when I traveled to New Delhi to catch up.

To conclude, Mansie is a super admissions consultant, aside from being a fantastic person to know and work with. Given her veteran-like experience in the field, her new book is a must read for anyone aspiring to join a world beating B-School!

Pranav Sharma, *2015 admit,* ***INSEAD***

*****

Being a re-applicant was challenging for me as I already had the taste of rejection. A global MBA from US is a dream that I cultivated since my undergrad days. So, after working for two years, I decided to give it a shot. But all my hard work was focused on GMAT and building my resume. I applied to a few universities, only to receive rejections from all of them, although I did manage to get interview call from some. I never realized what was wrong with me.

Anyway, I did not lose hope and decided to re-apply the next year. However, I was cautious this time, and decided to take help from an admission consultant. During this process, I met Mansie from Mansie Dewan Consulting. My heart and mind began to trust her when she informed me that she herself guides and coaches the applicant throughout the process. So I decided to take help from Mansie, and perhaps it was one of the best decisions that I ever made

Her way of knowing an applicant, both through face-to-face talk (skype in my case) and through Questionnaires made me very comfortable to express myself, both in written and oral form. Even if I missed anything to discuss during our appointment, I could call or write her, and she would reply promptly.

After having discussions with her several times, I could realize that I never expressed myself in the essays last year, which it was a big mistake. Mansie's biggest ability is that she can spot out strengths and weaknesses very easily, and she was never tired of encouraging me during the entire process. After a thorough discussion with her, I decided to apply to Tepper, Smeal, Broad, Krannert, Carey, Fisher, and Carlson. I managed to get interview calls from each of them, except Tepper.

Perhaps the biggest help I got from Mansie was during the interview process. We had countless number of mock interviews, and every time she helped me fix the smallest of errors. I realized that even though I had tremendous leadership experience, I was not good at quantifying my experience and achievements. She even let other persons take my mock interviews so that I felt comfortable. This experience made me confident when I took the actual interview. Eventually, I got admitted to Krannert and made my mind to go there as it is one of the best schools for Operations. She is the 2nd person, after my parent, who I called to inform about my admit because of all the guidance I received during the entire process. I would encourage everyone who reads this to work with Mansie Dewan because investing in Mansie Dewan Consultancy will yield nothing but profit in the end (even if you think like a businessman). I wish her all the best!

Prasenjit Datta, *Purdue Krannert Admit; CO 2017*

*****

Mansie had been with me through every step of my MBA application process. Once I had decided that I wanted to do an MBA, she helped me identify which schools would help me accentuate my strengths and which would be the ones best suited to the career goals I had in the short and long-term.

She reviewed my essays and coached me about how to make them stand out from amongst those of other applicants, at highly competitive schools, by ensuring that my strengths and weaknesses were reflected clearly and my essays communicated the best image of myself as a person to the school. She guided me in selecting the right life experiences to put in my essays. She reviewed my essays, resume and gave me mock interviews. Her coaching helped me have an individual approach to each school and I got into my top choice of school.

One piece of advice I would give to Indian MBA aspirants is to present the best version of yourself to each school, in accordance with what you want for yourself and what the school offers. This would involve some prioritization. I think this book will help you in tailoring your essays and profile to the school of your choice so that relevant achievements are highlighted to the admissions committees of those schools.

Ashok Harinarayanan, *Tepper CO 2016*

*****

Testimonials

I wanted to do an MBA from a premier B-School, but was clueless about how to get there, how to go about the application, etc. Mansie and her book not only forced me to think harder about all the "whys" before directly jumping on the "hows", but also completely changed my perspective towards a B-School application. She surely has lot of great insights on the process and her unique approach towards applications helps applicants to bring out the best in them and thus makes them stand out in the crowd. One very important thing I learnt from her is that every person is unique in himself or herself and comprise of both personal and professional experiences; it is therefore imperative that we include both in our application to make it truly unique and interesting. After step by step guiding through the basics of B-School application in her previous book, she seems to be taking it to a whole new level with her latest book. I hope this book proves as helpful to the readers as the first one was for me!

Shankey Poddar, *ISB CO 2016, recipient of INR 5 Lac scholarship*

*****

From knowing nothing about the admission process (except that writing GMAT is mandatory), to landing an admit in Germany's number 1 B-School, that was my journey which would not have been possible without Mansie's assistance. Helping to compose beautiful essays, of course, is something she is an expert at, but her guidance doesn't stop here. Mansie was there with me at every step of the application, from writing an email to the Admissions Committee, to preparing for an interview. She helped and guided me in the right direction. Be it making an appealing resume or finalizing the schools which meet my needs, Mansie's knowledge and expertise in every field were extraordinary. I am confident, with her new book, she will be helping other aspirants like me to realize their goals and maximize their potential.

Ashish Mehta, *2015 admit, Mannheim Business School, Germany*

*****

Today, when I look back past one-and-a-half years, I realize that the journey of GMAT and the application to the B-Schools was not more than a roller coaster ride. When I recall about my essay preparation, the only name which comes to mind is MANSIE Mam. Although I have not taken any essay preparation services from her, I followed her continuously from mid-2013 till 2014 end. Her book "Destination MBA" I bought in 2013 and I read it twice, thrice or may be multiple times. The language was so simple that it felt as if she herself was guiding me. Any doubt coming to my mind was immediately resolved by the next sentence. I read it so much that the book is now filled with underlines and highlighted texts. I even followed Mansie Mam's posts on pagalguy. I used to login there only to see what feedback she had given to other aspirants. This was not enough; I even followed her on radio. Although the timing was quite early, but I managed somehow. Also, not to forget, whenever I had some minor doubts about essay prep, I used to drop her a mail regarding that. She not only cleared my doubts, but also gave some extra suggestions about the same. Today she may not know me well, but for me she was the person to whom I can give complete credit for my Essay prep! :)

Tushar Khatri

*****

A book is only as good as its author. Mansie's timely help and her approach imbibed much needed confidence. Her clarity of thoughts and ability to understand nitty-gritties of the subject is reflected in her writings. While strongly recommending her first book, the second book is even better. Take the best out of it.

Alok A. Jahagirdar, *IIMC Admit 2015*

*****

Hello Mansie,

I would like to start by wishing you and your family a very happy new year! I just wanted to let you know that I got selected for the Masters in Advanced Finance (MIAF) course at IE and I will be heading there before the end of this month. I'm in the process of working out the loan and visa. I wanted to take the opportunity to thank you for handing me your book at the QS MBA Fair 2 years back. I have referred back to it numerous times during my application and interview process, and it has been a great guide all along. Thanks a lot for your help!

Do let me know if you ever decide to visit Madrid with your family in the coming year. It would be great to catch up.

Abhishek Jhunjhunwala, *IE Masters in Advanced Finance*

*****

The most important thing when making the decision to do your MBA is how you see yourself when you graduate. It is very important to map your career and your aspirations that will help you make three important decisions:
1. Whether I should go for an MBA?
2. What school should I go to for an MBA?
3. What should my story be?

All these questions need to be answered and cannot be answered without the help of proper guidance and that's where this book will help students. A lot of material out there deals with fluffy, intangible information. But this book can help with specific targeted feedback to hopeful aspirants looking to make an impact in their careers and the organization they will represent in the future.

Abhimanyu Lamba, *Richard Ivey, CO 2016*

*****

I remember the time when I was planning to apply to universities in UK and firmly believed that hitting the GMAT was the key. My belief, undoubtedly, was WRONG. Soon after giving my GMAT, I realized that what would matter in the end is a complete-package-application. It was during this time, after having done weeks of online research and speaking to a dozen alumni, I came up with a list of consultants with MDC on the top. I called up Mansie maam, fixed up an appointment for the next day, met her, discussed my profile, heard her approach on working on applications, and, believe me, I never saw that list again.

During that meeting, she took all the inputs from me and then swiftly dug out what was left. And not just that, she even counseled me and made sure that my choices and decisions do the best for me.

Once you begin working on your applications with her, you realize how novel her way of working is and feel more assured with each step you take ahead with her. She does not simply review your applications, but takes you along, through each and every word of it. She digs out the minutest of details from you, just to ensure that the best is offered at the end of the day. The best part of the entire process of my applications with her was not just getting through some of the best B-Schools, but getting to know myself even better.

Her second book will give you an insight on what the application demands, how you need to work upon it, how you need to work upon yourself before working on an application and much more. It gives you an inside view of how Mansie Dewan works, on what ideology does she work and how and what she expects the applicants to work upon for the applications.

Reading this book is going to comprehensively educate you on the application process and beyond. It's the best investment you'll make towards your future career.

Tejvir Singh, 2015 *admit, Manchester Business School, Cranfield, City University Cass and Warwick*

*****

I had thought that "Destination MBA" was a complete and a perfect read and that nothing could better it. Although this amazing and a must read book was the only reason I approached Mansie for consultation, I never knew what was in store for me until I started working with her. For me, Mansie has been like a painter with a white board and the magical brush. Mansie is inspirational, motivating, very hardworking and yes, always available. (We have had discussions at 3 am in the night). She is the "ideal thought leader" you would require to cross the admission hurdle. She not only helps you carve out the most beautiful essays out of a few bulleted points you have, but also has the ability to make you better in thought and idea structuring, a true coach!!

Most special is the relationship that Mansie shared with me. I was not just another client; her level of engagement imbibed trust and confidence that was unheard of. Such a relationship helped adding real value to the essays. Once in that relationship, you would never know how the most candid of discussions were meant to seep out valuable information from you, adding to your application. This is true for all her clients!

One thing's for sure that if you are looking for a ready-made cooked up essay suiting your face, don't come to Mansie. However, if you are ready for the journey of a lifetime, if you really need the MBA and are ready to work towards it and if you are ready to be pestered for good — Mansie Dewan is the name to reach out to!

Mohit Khullar, *2015 admits to UCLA Anderson and University of Texas Mccombs with $40k Scholarship*

*****

Following Mansie's guidance to prepare for my dream college for Masters in Management was like a journey of self-discovery; not only could I build an eye catching resume, but also write an impactful Statement of Purpose, reflecting all my achievements in an effective manner. With Mansie's guidance, I could provide effective details of my academic and industrial experience to help my recommenders to write highly effective recommendations for me. I am sure the book will be very helpful to all the aspirants to prepare for their dream university

Yash Kaushik, 2015 *admit, Masters of Engineering Management, Northwestern University*

*****

STRATEGIES TO GET YOU STARTED

If you've bought this book, chances are that you either have doubts or fears or both in relation to your MBA journey. The difference between the two is that you can clear your doubts by getting more information, but nobody can take the fear out of you, except yourself!

Getting an MBA admission requires strategic planning and focus. The question of how to go about the entire process looms large in the minds of many young aspirants. The first hurdle is profiling yourself and includes choosing the right colleges, taking into consideration your goals — what YOU are looking from an MBA program. Many MBA aspirants get their profile evaluated by multiple consultants. Each consultant has their own approach and perspective. Different evaluations can create doubts in the aspirant's mind, which can hamper their own judgment. Remember guys, you are your own profiler and strategist. I will not talk you out of seeking free evaluations from multiple sources, but take each advice with a pinch of salt and use your own discretion. Having done your own research makes you stronger and confident about your case. And before you begin, you should definitely cover the following:

Perfection is a time bound process. Start as early as you can to achieve Success.

- Identify what you seek out of an MBA education — both professionally and personally.
- Make a list of your activities, achievements (professional and personal) and skills.
- Make a list of all the important and meaningful experiences in your life and think about how they have shaped your personality and thought process.
- Make a list of all your strengths and weaknesses and illustrate examples that demonstrate them.
- Discuss your most meaningful leadership experiences and what you learnt from them.

- What are some of the challenges you've faced in life? How have they shaped you as a person?
- What are the most distinguishing characteristics of your background, experiences and personality?

The whole rationale behind this exercise is to get a clarity on your profile and identify the reasons for wanting your MBA. We will discuss more about how you can present yourself impressionably through essays in the essay section, but now let's move on to how to identify and zero in on which programs to apply to.

Choosing your fit schools

Each business school has its strengths and offerings. You need to figure out what is personally more important to you and how each school can impact your career growth.

1. You can differentiate schools according to their academics and teaching methodology, specializations on offer, brand and their career services.
2. You might prefer to study at a certain geographic location because you want to build your career in that area. For example, ISB, IIMs, NUS, Nanyang are popular study choices for people wanting to work in the Asian region.
3. Look at schools that actively place students in the industry and function of your choice.

Based on what parameters are most important to you, you can start drafting a list of schools fitting your needs.

You should also rank your list in order of preference so that you're clear in your mind about which school to join in the situation that you have admits from more than one business school. In this case, you should be declining offers from schools that you will definitely not attend because you have an admission offer from your first choice school, or a huge financial incentive from another (in form of scholarships, fee waivers, stipends, etc.). This will allow admissions teams to consider the other waiting aspirants and keep their wait short!

While shortlisting schools, it is important is to keep those schools that are likely to want you as part of their class in your kitty. Your applications should be submitted to at least 3 of such schools that you want to attend and are likely to accept you. To zero in on your targets, visit the class profile sections and check the backgrounds, qualifications and experience of admitted students. If it is similar to yours, and the school's curriculum, placement record, teaching methodology excite you, then go for it!

In order to submit your applications smoothly and seamlessly, I recommend that you generate a list of your target schools even before taking the GMAT/GRE. Not only will you be prepared well in time to structurally prepare yourself for your target GMAT/GRE score according to the average score of the school, but you will save yourself a lot of money by selecting to send your scores to your top five choices when you take the exam. Also, with so many programs on offer, it might get a little confusing to narrow your choices to just 5-6 close to the applications deadlines, leaving you very little time in preparation to demonstrate a good fit between yourself and the program.

Should you rely solely on rankings?

Rankings, by all means, can be the beginning of your shortlisting search, but you do not want to solely base your decision on these. Most rankings are surveys and data which help students to compare schools on various criteria like reputation, recruiter satisfaction, average GMAT/GRE scores, but are not measures of the educational quality of the institutions. Course offerings are different from school to school and individual criteria and personal expectations of a student vary, so an excellent "fit" school for one might not even be on the list of another. This is why there is no substitute to doing your own, detailed research. Randomly choosing schools just based on rankings can lead to disappointment later.

What you should really do

There is nothing better than conducting a detailed research after narrowing down a couple of schools. Start looking closely at school websites, research on the curriculum and faculty and try making personal connections with these schools either through direct contact, through fairs, virtual information sessions or current students and alumni.

Pay very close attention to the companies hiring at your target schools. Many offer complete employment reports on their websites but in case they don't, you can always reach out to their career development centres directly. They are always happy to help.

Scrutinize the target program and each of its components. Also look at extracurricular activities on offer and see if these are in sync with your educational needs. Remember, the school should appeal to you on a professional and personal level and you need to be 100% convinced of your choice.

Utilize every opportunity to interact with current students and alumni to get first hand perspectives on the quality of the course and its impact on their personal and professional lives. An insider's peep will also help you decipher if the school's values are in sync with your own. Lastly, do not miss any opportunity to visit the school campus, if possible. You will probably not get any bonus points on account of having made the effort, but the preparedness and thoroughness will definitely reflect in the quality of your application and interview, taking you a bit closer to your ultimate goal.

STAND UP AND GET YOURSELF NOTICED

Features of your profile to help you decide on your target schools

Academics: Your undergraduate and graduate GPA or percentage, past academic record and the GMAT/GRE scores are important components that will help you choose schools. And be very pragmatic here; you need a stellar academic record and the required GMAT/GRE score to target the top schools. A weak undergraduate collegiate result may hamper your chances, but there is scope to improve your performance during graduation or compensate it through an above average GMAT/GRE score. Some schools also require international applicants to take the TOEFL, so it is best to get this very easy part of the process over and done with as soon as possible!

Work Experience: Business schools like to know about your career growth, leadership positions you've handled, increase in responsibilities over time and ability to manage teams effectively. If you have not had significant growth in the recent past, you may still have time to take on new leadership positions (on the work and extracurricular front) and increase your job responsibilities. Think about your strengths and weaknesses. Think of ways to overcome your weaknesses and earnestly start working on them. A minimum of two years of experience is expected by most business schools, but check the class profile of your target schools to know the average.

Goals: Are your post MBA career goals a good fit with the mission and offerings of your target school? You need to think deeply and develop a concrete list of goals in sync with the school's offerings and ability to place you in the target industry and function, post MBA.

Extracurricular activities: This deserves a special mention, as a lot of Indian applicants find themselves wanting in this area. Extracurricular involvements not only distinguish an applicant from the rest of the pool, but also demonstrate that he or she has well rounded and holistic personality and can balance their time well.

Extracurricular involvements imply that you can balance an academic/professional life with your hobbies and interests and will continue to do so throughout your life. Incidentally, these activities also help you choose your schools, in terms of the extracurricular involvement opportunities that your target school offers.

Preparing for the GMAT

Giving the GMAT is the First Major Milestones in your MBA journey. It determines whether you have the academic tenacity to participate in a rigorous MBA program. Generally, Indians (read: Engineers or professionals from technical backgrounds) are naturally high GMAT scorers so the competition is high!

There are different ways to prepare for the test and what works for one might not work for another. You first need to figure out if you're the sort of person who can study yourself or you need a formal GMAT training course. To begin with, visit www.mba.com and download the free GMAT practice software. Your performance in the first practice test will be a good indicator of your current standing. If you are close to your target GMAT score, then self-preparation might be the best option for you. If you need lots of improvement, then think along the lines of joining a formal preparatory course or some online tutoring.

Regardless of whether you prepare on your own or join a course, it is crucial to develop a systemized study plan and practice regularly. You could purchase a few books (Manhattan, Kaplan and Veritas Preparation are popular choices) and reference online resources. There are plenty of online preparation companies, too. Your books or study materials should be your best friends at this point of time.

The key to success is consistency in your preparation and regular practice. With dedicated efforts, even if you have been an average student all through your academic life, you can crack the GMAT and get your target score. After all, a high GMAT will strengthen your application package exponentially.

What it entails

The GMAT Exam has four sections — Analytical Writing Assessment (AWA), Integrated Reasoning (IR), Quantitative Aptitude (Quant) and Verbal Aptitude (Verbal).

1. Analytical Writing Assessment section requires the test taker to write a 30 minute essay, either strengthening or weakening a given argument. The purpose of the AWA section is to check your writing skills and ability to give logical arguments to support your opinions.
2. The Integrated Reasoning section requires the test taker to solve 12 questions in 30 minutes. The questions are based on graphs and tables and generally need quick analysis of tons of data. The purpose of this section is to check your data analysis skills.
3. The Quantitative Aptitude section has 37 questions, to be solved in 75 minutes. The questions are based on high school mathematics concepts in arithmetic, algebra and geometry etc.
4. The Verbal Aptitude section has 41 questions, to be solved in 75 minutes. The questions in this section are based on your understanding of the usage of the English language and on your reasoning ability when presented with an argument.

Overall, the GMAT exam tests your English communication, reasoning and mathematical skills, which are critical to pursue a course, and subsequently a career, in management.

Understanding the scoring

The GMAT Exam gives the test taker a total score and individual sectional scores.

The AWA sectional score is out of 6.0 in increments of 0.5. So, a test taker may get a score of 4.5 or 5.0 but not 5.25. The essay written by the test taker is evaluated by multiple test evaluators and the average of their scores is the overall score.

The IR sectional score is out of 8. This section is not adaptive. It is based on the number of correct responses given by the test taker.

The Quant sectional score is based on the number of correct and incorrect responses. It is an adaptive section — so if the test taker answers a question correctly, his or her score goes up and the next question asked is of a higher difficulty level; if the test taker answers a question incorrectly, the score goes down and the next question asked if of a lower difficulty level. The Quant sectional score is out of 60. The maximum score achieved currently is 51.

The Verbal sectional score marking is done exactly like the Quant and is also out of a 60. The maximum score achieved is 51.

The scaled scores of Quant and Verbal are used to calculate the composite score, which is out of 800. Scores which are 760+ are 99 percentile. IR and AWA scores are not considered in calculating the composite score. After the GMAT exam, the candidate gets an unofficial score card. It contains:

1. IR score and percentile
2. Scaled Quant Score and percentile
3. Scaled Verbal score and percentile
4. Composite score and percentile

The AWA score and percentile come with the official score card and are available after 15 to 20 days of the test date.

Preparation

The ideal time to start preparing for the GMAT is 3 to 6 months ahead of the date on which you want to take the test (i.e. the test date). This period is dependent on how much time you can devote on a weekly basis and on your present level—which will decide how much content you need to cover.

Before beginning, you should take a mock diagnostic GMAT test. This will give you cues about your strengths and weaknesses, giving you an excellent starting point, knowing exactly where to concentrate your efforts.

It is advisable to take at least 10 to 20 full length mock GMAT Exams towards the end of your preparation.

What study material do you need?

There are many study guides and books available for the GMAT.

The study material can be broadly divided into two categories—mandatory and optional.

The following resources are recommended:

i. The Official Guide for GMAT Review: This book is the GMAT bible. It is the official book released by the makers of the GMAT exam—Graduate Management Admission Council (GMAC). The content given in the Official Guide (OG) is the most authentic content released. Previous years' papers are not released for the GMAT. This is the book on which you can rely for retired GMAT questions. The book is designed in a way that even a layperson can thoroughly understand the content. You need to do all the questions in this book at least twice or thrice.

ii. The Official Guide for GMAT Verbal Review: This book contains additional Verbal questions. It is also released by the GMAC, hence, has authentic GMAT content. You need to do all the questions in this at least twice.

iii. The Official Guide for GMAT Quant Review: This book contains additional Quant questions. Again, solve all of them twice.

Please note: It is advisable to practice official questions, as doing so builds a perspective for the very kind of questions that are frequently tested by GMAC.

Apart from these official resources, the resources mentioned below are also great for extra prep:

Manhattan GMAT Sentence Correction Strategy Guide: An excellent source for the Grammar and the Sentence Correction sections.

Manhattan GMAT Foundations of GMAT Verbal: This book takes care of the Verbal section.

Powerscore Critical Reasoning Bible: This book is for students who are weak in Critical Reasoning section.

Aristotle RC 99: This book provides 99 RCs which are good in quality for practice.

The following books are optional:

Some students need help in one or more sections that they feel challenged in. In such cases, one or more of the following books can be used to overcome their weaknesses:

    i. High School Math Books: These books are those that were completed from 6th grade to 10th grade — only the topics relevant to the exam need to be studied.

    ii. GMAT CLUB Math Book: This is for students who face difficulty in the Quant section of the exam.

    iii. High School English Grammar by Wren and Martin: This is to be used only for reference and to study some areas of English grammar that are challenging for the particular student.

There is no dearth of books and guides for the GMAT exam in the market. But your time is limited and the above mentioned books are more than sufficient to take care of all sections of the exam.

After you have completed the above mentioned study material, the following practice tests and extra sectional practice are recommended:

    i. GMATPrep Software: This software can be downloaded for free from mba.com post registration. This contains around 100 Questions and 2 CATs (Computer Adaptive Tests)

    ii. GMATPrep Question Pack 1: This software bundle needs to be purchased and can be integrated to the GMATPrep Software. It increases the questions which can be practised to 400.

    iii. GMATPrep Exam Pack 1: This software bundle needs to be purchased and can be integrated into the GMATPrep Software. It increases the number of CATs in GMATPrep by 2. So after installing this pack, there will be 4 CATs and all these CATs are composed of retired GMAT questions.

iv. The Score 800 Tests: Available at www.score800.com

v. Manhattan Prep GMAT Tests: One free CAT is available at www.manhattangmat.com. The rest of the practice tests can be purchased at www.manhattangmat.com

vi. VeritasPrep GMAT CATs: One free CAT is available at VeritasPrep.com and the rest of the practice tests can be purchased.

vii. Economist GMAT: One free CAT is available at gmat.economist.com.

Course completion plan

The course completion plan for different students varies as per their schedule. So, each person needs to draw up their own schedule—an absolute must before starting the preparation.

Total number of study hours needed before you start testing: 120 to 150 hours.

Total number of weeks needed before you start testing: 9 to 12 weeks.

INTERVIEW WITH THE GMAC

The following are GMAC's responses to the questions presented by me. Ms. Jennifer Garfinkel, Director, Media Relations, and one of the official spokespersons for the Graduate Management Admission Council answers:

How will GMAC advise a complete newbie to go about the GMAT preparation?

Familiarizing yourself with the concepts and skills tested in the GMAT and the test structure and format would be the first step. A diagnostic or practice test, such as the one found in the GMATPrep or the Official Guide, provides a good starting baseline. This can help guide and focus the test taker's preparation, based on their personal areas of strength and weakness. Practicing the different questions types and taking GMAT practice tests helps a test taker continue to improve their skills and achieve their personal best.

The mba.com website offers a GMAT Prep Timeline to help prepare your study plan (including tips, products, advice and resources), recognizing that every individual has a different learning style. It is advisable to design a study plan that fits with your lifestyle, pace, learning goals and timing.

What is the importance of both the AWA and IR in the exam and the overall application? (There is a lot of confusion regarding this)

Schools use multiple sources of information to make admissions decisions. This is true of both non-exam sources — such as work experience, undergraduate major and academic performance, recommendations, application essays, etc., as well as sources of information within the exam and its different sections, which test different skills. Each of the GMAT sections provides unique information about candidates' abilities that might not be otherwise apparent from these other sources. One of the benefits of the Analytical Writing section is, that in addition to the score, schools are provided with the essay, which allows them to glimpse the writing style of the candidate, and some schools have said that it is useful to evaluate the fluency of non-native English speakers. The Integrated Reasoning section resonates with schools and with employers because the question formats resemble the types of tasks that would be required in business school and in businesses.

Ultimately, however, each program will decide on the emphasis to be placed on any of the admission factors based on the needs of the program and the history of students within their own programs.

Is there any disadvantage of cancelling the score?

There could be some disadvantages for the test taker. One is that the person loses the opportunity to tell his/her story. If you retake the GMAT and score significantly higher, you have lost the opportunity to visibly highlight this accomplishment to the admissions committee. You may be able to regain this opportunity by painting a picture of the hard work, discipline and tenacity it took to improve your score via the schools' essays or interview — but your argument would be strengthened by having your scores reflected on your official GMAT score report. Another disadvantage is that you may miss the opportunity to highlight HIGHER sub-scores. Schools tend to look at both the total GMAT score and the sub-scores. Of course, should you choose to re-instate cancelled scores within 60 days, you are able to address the two disadvantages just listed.

Are multiple GMAT attempts frowned upon by business schools?

No. Most schools look to our highest score as an indicator of your skills. Schools also look at the individual sub-scores from multiple tests to get a sense of your true capabilities. Taking the exam a second (or third) time if you did not perform up to your abilities on the first exam, will not only likely improve your score, but shows the admissions committee you are willing to make the extra effort to learn something new, demonstrate your competency or command of the fundamental skills necessary to succeed in B-School and put your best application forward.

What are some of the factors (external and internal) that affect performance during the exam? (Note: Our response is based on general standardized testing experiences, not necessarily the GMAT exam itself)

Standardized testing is not something that people experience every day, so several outside factors may affect performance. The environment is designed for security, but going to an unfamiliar place for a high stakes purpose can be daunting for some. The format of the exam, such as question types and timing, may not be familiar. These issues — the testing environment and the testing format — may resolve themselves with proper preparation. The GMAT Handbook gives candidates the idea of what to expect at the test center. The official GMATPrep resources not only provide information on the types of questions, but have full length practice tests that mirror the testing experience.

Research suggests that some personality factors, such as risk-aversion may affect standardized test performance. For instance, someone who is reluctant to guess, who wants to be absolutely certain their answer is right, can run into trouble on a standardized test when they run out of time. Test anxiety is another factor that may affect performance. In some cases, the anxiety is related to the unfamiliar circumstances described above, and those more familiar with the test and the expected environment may have reduced anxiety.

All of these factors taken into consideration, it cannot be overstated that preparation and familiarity are the keys to success and both common sense and rigorous research confirm the advantage of taking the time to prepare.

Is it advisable to refer to multiple sources for preparation? Generally, I have observed that the highest scorers tend to restrict themselves to the OG.

Research on standardized testing suggests that the best test preparation is that which mirrors the testing experience. For the GMAT exam, the practice tests on GMATPrep would be the best source. Also, any product that has *real* GMAT questions would serve as good preparation, which means that the Official Guide is also a good resource.

WORKING ON THE RESUME

It is said that "The first impression is the last impression." This holds especially true for your MBA applications. The resume is the first thing the admissions committee will look at, before moving on to your other documents. It is important to ensure that this first impression lasts and a look at your resume enthuses your application reviewer to look forward to the other sections.

Ideally, the resume should be a summary of all your professional accomplishments and highlights in one page. The resume gets less than a minute's attention, so all the salient features of your profile should be clearly evident. Every point should count and show the admissions committee the strengths of your profile.

Strategies for creating a strong MBA application resume. Let's discuss them one by one.

1. *It needs to be easy on the eyes*

The golden rule for creating a business school resume is that it should be easy to read and comprehend. Within a page, you also need to ensure ample white spaces. The design needs to be simple and unpretentious. The font needs to be simple too—Times Roman is my choice. No curvy, snaky lettering please. Stick to a traditional style and use a font size of 10 minimum.

2. *Limit it to one page*

The only exception to this rule is when you have more than 8 to 10 years of work experience. While many schools will accept two page resumes, their preference clearly is for a one page. As an applicant, you do not want to subject them to lengthy prose and should respect their time. With so many applications to go through, they will certainly appreciate the extra effort you made to make your profile summary as concise as possible.

3. Avoid technical jargon

You are creating a resume for a business school application, not for a job change. Your resume needs to avoid all technical jargon, as well as programs and skills that you might otherwise include in your resume if you were looking for a job switch in your industry. The resume should be a meaningful synopsis of your professional history, progression and progress. It is the document that clearly showcases a connect between your work experiences and other experiences and your goals.

4. Focus on accomplishments and impact

Career progression and impact on employer are what admissions committees are looking for. A simple description of job responsibilities won't contribute to your cause. When your job title is descriptive of what your work is, why waste a bullet point in describing the work you do? For example, as an Operations Manager in a manufacturing plant, you are expected to oversee smooth operations and execution. Why write it down? Or if you're a business analyst, it is implied that you analyze business problems and suggest solutions. No need to dedicate space to mention it separately. Quite simply, neither your job title, nor the description of the work that you did will set you apart. What will do so is the kind of achievements and impact you had, while holding that position.

Quantify the impact you had, giving figures if possible. Your contribution may have:
  a. saved money for your company
  b. generated revenue
  c. saved time in a critical time bound project
  d. arrested attrition
  e. brought in repeat business, etc.

How many people did you lead? What strategy did you adopt? Don't be vague; be very specific. Give details.

5. Highlight leadership

Many of you might argue about how you can demonstrate leadership when you haven't got a chance to be in a leadership position. Well, it's not just about the position you hold and what you can do formally, it is also about making use of each and every opportunity to add value to your employer.

Leadership can demonstrated in many different ways. You can be formally in-charge of a specific project to contribute tangibly. Or you can grab hold of an opportunity that presents itself, to show that you have the potential. Almost always, leadership is about working well with people, so leadership and team skills invariably go hand in hand. When you think about it in this way, you will realise that you will definitely have at least a few experiences to demonstrate your leadership, whether or not you've formally been in charge.

6. Begin each bullet point with a verb

An action packed resume always has the maximum punch. Don't ever use the word "responsible", rather, begin your point with an actionable verb to show that you are a dynamic individual, who is always in charge and ready for some action. Some examples of verbs that you can use are:

- Accomplished
- Facilitated
- Led
- Evaluated
- Designed
- Contributed
- Developed
- Assisted
- Implemented
- Documented
- Organized

- Designated
- Monitored
- Negotiated
- Conceptualized
- Optimized

7. Give the maximum importance to your most recent work experience

Devote maximum space to your most recent experiences. There's a very good reason for this. Your current experiences relate best with your post MBA goals and these are the very experiences that help you describe and present yourself. Use space for earlier stints judiciously and do not devote more than 2-3 bullet points for each one. If you've recently changed jobs and do not have much to speak about your current employer, then it's fair to dedicate more space to the earlier experience. However, remember — the key is to talk about achievements and impact.

For the earlier stints, especially the ones right after college, don't dedicate more than 2 bullet points to each.

8. Always put your educational experience after the professional experience

Your professional experience always comes first, especially if you have more than 2 years experience after graduating. Start with your most noteworthy and important experiences, followed by the others, in reverse chronological order. This is followed by Education, Extracurriculars and interests.

9. Finally, edit your draft and edit until you are satisfied that this is the best you can do to make each and every section say something about you.

A few common errors to avoid
1. Writing extensive prose as if you are writing your life history.
2. Going onto a second page without good reason to do so.
3. Making up stuff or fibbing.
4. Including articles and pronouns which is a precious waste of words and space
5. Using overused and clichéd terms like "Dynamic", "self-motivated " or "multitasker"
6. Over using action words
7. Forgetting or botching-up the dates and timelines
8. Providing irrelevant and personal information, like marital status and birthday
9. Including a separate line for "objective" at the beginning
10. Using designs and fancy fonts

The following resumes are for reference purpose only. The data is not reflective of the aspirant's work or companies mentioned.

PIYUSH JAIN

Flat AX, Block *, Krishnanagar Apartments,
+919740XXXXXX
Vimanapura, HAL, Bangalore — 560017, India
piyush.jain@outlook.com

PROFESSIONAL EXPERIENCE

Consultant, Deloitte Consulting, Bangalore, India, Jun 2011–Present

The role involves working closely with global clients to understand their business requirements, translate them into technical solutions, and present relevant and timely solutions in response to current and emerging business needs.

System Integration Project ($ 5.2 Billion Technology Client) Feb 2014–Present

- Leading a module to **reduce** accounting costs to **60%** by replacing existing accounting application
- Standardized client knowledge transfer process for **>40 modules**; implemented *Wiki page* module snapshots
- Conceptualized a *Reward & Recognition* program for a **team of 75+** for internal project awards

Procurement Analytics Project ($ 2.4 Billion Industrial Products Client) Jun 2013–Dec 2013

- Led a team for 1 out of the 3 major modules; involved in end-to-end client delivery of Procurement module
- Spearheaded solution and knowledge transfer to client during the support phase for a period of >30 days

Financial and HR Analytics ($ 7.2 Billion Engineering and Construction Client) Aug 2012–Jun 2013
- Implemented Financial and Human Resources Business-Reporting for an organization with 27,000 employees
- Published a white paper for service line CoE showcasing a new method in financial business reporting
- Received an award from the Lead Engagement Partner and a personal handwritten letter of appreciation

Real Estate Analytics ($ 2 Billion Real Estate client) Sep 2011–Apr 2012
- Used BI reporting platform to create business reports on customer management, acquisitions and disposals

PROFESSIONAL ACCOMPLISHMENTS
- **SME** on Data visualization Tools; trained **more than 100** professionals across hierarchies on the same
- Developed Data Visualization application for **Oil and Gas** client proposal for location-wise well operations
- Created application to determine patient characteristics and product distribution details for **Healthcare** client
- Conceptualized and conducted training series for **30 practitioners** on Business Information Modeling
- Among five percent Business Technology Analysts to get promoted to the position of Consultant with a top rating
- Awarded Best Buddy in Service Line for facilitating trainings at Boot Camp and mentoring new recruits

EDUCATION

Aug 2006–Jul 2011

- *Indian Institute of Technology (IIT) Madras*: Bachelor & Master of Technology, Mechanical Engg. (CGPA: 6.8/10)

POSITIONS OF RESPONSIBILITY

- Managed campus relations with IIT Madras for Deloitte Consulting during the placements of 2012–13
- Elected as **Technical Affairs Secretary** of a 300-member hostel; founded the first robotics club, 2008–09
- Selected as a Quality Management System coordinator (out of 100+ applicants) for *Saarang*, the Annual Cultural Festival of IIT Madras involving 1000+ colleges in Jan 2009
- Supervised a 30-member External Publicity team covering 8 states for the Cultural festival, 2008–09
- **Placement Representative** for 200+ students; responsible for placements and company relations, 2009–10
- Sponsorship Publicity Coordinator for *Saarang* 2008; managed publicity efforts for companies like Nokia etc.

EXTRACURRICULAR (SPORTS & CSR)

- Captain of the Deloitte Consulting Service Line Football team from Aug 2011 to present
- Captained Hostel Hockey team to its **First Gold Medal** in five years in inter hostel tournaments in 2009–10
- Led a team of 80 practitioners during Deloitte's Annual Community Initiative, "Impact Day 2013"
- Led a team of 15 practitioners during Impact Day 2012. Team worked with the NGO "One Billion Literates Foundation" in providing English education at government primary schools

ASHISH RASTOGI

999, R. N. Tagore Road, Boro Pukur, Bediapara, Dum Dum,
Kolkata, West Bengal — 700077, India
Phone: (+91) 9853XXXXXX
Mail: XXXXX@gmail.com

PROFESSIONAL EXPERIENCE

Tata Steel Limited, KPO, Odisha

Manager Projects (Design)
Aug 2013–Present

- Developing the Product Lifecycle Management platform for the department and integrating it into departmental operations. The initiative aims at developing a plant-maintenance and planning tool in 3-D.

- Co-leading a team of 6 in the design cell and working directly with Tata Steel's technology partners Tata Growth Shop, iDesign and PTC.

- Overseeing engineering drawing review, 2-D to 3-D conversion, design assemblies of major processes, creation and management of equipment database and coordinating transfer of information to and from the department.

- Attained lowest design-assembly time for major sub-assemblies while working independently and again when working with I-Design.

- Achieved highest 2D-to-3D conversion rate as a part of the newly formed design team within one month.

Manager Projects (Mechanical)
Jul 2012–Jul 2013

- Managed the supply, erection and commissioning of two heavy equipment packages for the Raw Material Handling Systems (RMHS) department.
- Coordinated equipment delivery, inspection and billing cycles between two suppliers, the Costing & Finance section and project consultants Dastur & Co. during the supply phase.
- Mitigated the effects of a scheduling error which did not take into account the impending monsoons, by reducing a projected delay of over 2 months to about 25–26 days by convincing contract companies to share resources.
- Coordinated with the central Project Management Office and created a simple yet secure online project management portal in RMHS for real-time progress assessment and reporting purposes.

Tata Steel Limited, Jamshedpur Works

Management Trainee (Technical)
Jul 2011–Jun 2012

- Independently worked on a project in the Tubes division to design a prototype which has a cost saving potential of $2 Million. The same idea has been granted a patent by the Indian Patent Office.
- Undertook a TQM project. Recommended two separate ways to improve the lifecycle of a component by a factor of 4.
- Acclimatised with the Marketing & Sales division and met with several Tata Steel customers to understand the business relationships of the company, both within and outside the country, and to understand how the B2B and B2C business methodologies are adopted.

- Participated in an Outbound Leadership Development program to learn about team building and leadership skills In Uttarkashi, India.

EDUCATION

Bachelor of Engineering, Mechanical Engineering, Jadavpur University, Kolkata, India, 2011
- CGPA: 8.39/10

EXTRACURRICULAR

- Co-Founder and Executive Member of Tata Steel's Music Club. The club has performed in major company events over the years and has organized music events like "Jamshedpur Unplugged" in recent times.
- Guitarist in the band "Blacksmiths" since 2011; have played bass, rhythm and fingerstyle-acoustic for a myriad of western and Indian songs.
- Completed all 3 levels of motorcycle race training course by Apex Racing Academy in Kari Motor Speedway, Coimbatore, India in Dec 2013.
- Organized events like Parichay, GT Rally, Mix-n-Match Cricket and other non-competitive events as part of the Cultural & Sports Committee of Management Trainee Batch of 2011.

Profiling, strategizing and building your essays

Competition is fierce at almost all leading business schools and seats for international applicants are limited. The Admissions Committee members reviewing your application will give it a few minutes and, in that time, you need to get their attention. Your application is what brings your profile to light and reveals your candidature and its fit with your target school.

In this limited and crucial time that you have, you need to convince them about wanting you on board. Whether it is through your work experience, extracurricular activities, community service or conspicuous background or a combination of these factors, you have to highlight the strength of your profile.

Preparing an MBA application involves literally breaking up your life into bite sized pieces, scrutinizing them and then re-assembling the important ones into a whole new marketable YOU.

Most business schools initially evaluate candidates by their intellectual strength (academic performance and GMAT/GRE scores). If these numbers meet the school's expectations, the application is further scrutinized to decipher the candidate's "fit" with the school.

So yes, dig deep and think hard!

- What is unique about your candidature? What is most important to you?
- Think about your school and college experiences. What comes to your mind?
- Think about most impressionable growing up experiences.

There are a few important common characteristics that an admissions committee is looking for. These are mentioned below, in no particular order:

- Potential for excellence
- Diversity in background and experience
- Strong leadership acumen

- Excellent interpersonal skills
- Team spirit, ability to lead and motivate teams and cohesively work as part of a team for common objectives.
- Vision and determination for a strong future for self
- Dynamic personality

Outstanding MBA applicants have a few things in common. One is that they are able to connect the dots between their past, present and future. They are also able to demonstrate a strong link between their passions and interests and their extracurricular pursuits. For example, if you claim that you feel passionate about education and how it can help eradicate unemployment, but have not supported any relevant cause, then your claim will ring false.

The importance of work experience

Though the GMAT/GRE scores and the academic performance are initial scrutiny criteria, the relevance of work experience cannot be undermined.

You need to show to the Admissions Committee that you have what it takes to both benefit from as well as contribute meaningfully to the MBA classroom. Group projects and team based activities are an integral aspect of the curriculum and you need to be able to draw meaningful insights from your past experiences and industry knowledge to these. You need to showcase that you have the ability to follow guidelines, work in high pressure situations, meet strict deadlines, organize yourself and work well in teams. Moreover, recruiters who come to campus seek experienced candidates, making work experience a mandatory requirement of the admission process.

Quality vs Quantity

Just meeting the bare minimum work experience criteria is not enough. There are candidates who are not ready for B-School until a few years into their careers and then there are others who are crystal clear in their thought process very early regarding how an MBA fits into the bigger scheme of things for them.

Maturity and clarity of thought process and relevance of past experience to post MBA goals is important—almost as important as the kind of impact the candidate has had on their organization(s). Often, the two are connected. Focused, self-motivated and dedicated aspirants tend to have a tangible effect on their companies, irrespective of the size and kind of company they work for. To say it simply, the quality of experience counts more than the number of years.

Personal Attributes

Reputed business schools value more than just work experience, grades and GMAT/GRE scores. They want their incoming students to be the hallmarks of the qualities that constitute a good leader. These students are future brand ambassadors for the school and choosing the right fit class is a very serious responsibility. Qualities that are most sought after are:

- Leadership
- Strong professional experience
- Integrity
- Teamwork
- Analytical ability
- Managerial ability
- Strong communication skills

How to craft impactful essays

Your essays are not the place to blatantly list off all your personal and professional accomplishments. Rather, through these, you show the Admissions Committee who you really are. You finally get to show that you are more than just an MBA applicant number, with a GMAT/GRE score, academics, and a professional background. Use the essays as your voice—show the Admissions Committee the unique aspects of your profile.

You can actually start planning for your essays even before the business schools release their essays prompts and deadlines. While the actual essays might differ, certain themes are evergreen and repeat year after year.

For example, your goals will not change, irrespective of which school you apply to. Neither will the diversity of your profile with which you will be able to contribute meaningfully to your cohort. You may also be asked about a challenging situation, a failure or to talk about your most meaningful leadership experiences or accomplishments.

Use the STAR approach

S — Situation   T — Task   A — Action   R — Result

This STAR model is widely used to prepare not just B-School essays, but also interviews. For your essays, when you conceptualize each experience, you should be able to identify the situation, the task you faced, the actions you took (and any challenges you faced along the way) and the result of your work.

The distinct details that you share will make your essays vibrant and unique and make you strike a chord with the admissions committee. Just like the sample essays shared in this book did. You might wonder what good reading these sample essays will do. My aim is give you inspiration to write well and achieve what you set out to do — grab the Admissions Committee's attention and invite you for interview.

Specific pointers: Here are the few things you should keep in mind while crafting your essays:

1. **Show, don't tell.** Don't be generic. The beauty of an essay is in details. Add vibrancy and specifics to your essays. This will make your essays attention grabbing and the readers will read them because they want to know more and not because they have to. Write about 20% more in your initial drafts. You can always edit and trim them later.

2. **Be structured in your approach.** Even though you will revise, refine and edit your drafts later (it's all

a very normal part of the process) you need a rough outline and plan for your essay. List down all the main points you intend to cover in your essay so you will know at the outset that your essay will have a beginning, a body and an ending. This will also ensure that you do not have any experiences to repeat in two different prompts of the same business school essays. With a map to follow, you are also more likely to adhere to the word limit.

3. **Answer the specific question asked.** This seems fairly simple to do. But believe me, it is very easy to deviate from the core question asked and move in a completely different tangent. Many applicants, with stellar academics, GMAT scores and experiences, sometimes have a difficult time sticking to the scope of the question asked.

4. **Make connections.** Don't just list a series of interconnected experiences, but make the relevant connections. The essay should flow from the beginning to the end, with context of what happened and why. What were the actions that you took and how did you feel? Share your apprehensions, excitement, happiness, or whatever other emotions you were feeling and discuss what you learnt. Without awareness and introspection, your essays will appear insipid.

5. **Review and revise.** Give yourself ample time to review the essay drafts multiple times and think about possible alternate approaches. How does the presentation look best? The process takes time and, sometimes, after sitting on a draft for days, you might come up with a completely new striking idea that takes the essay up several notches! You never know!

6. **Edit and proofread.** It is normal to revise and edit essays a couple of times till you are satisfied that you have given it your very best. Your essays should be well refined with no grammatical, spelling and punctuation errors and no use of superfluous words at the time you're ready to submit.

INTERVIEWS WITH ADMISSIONS COMMITTEES

Let's now have a look at the answers of a few business schools in response to the questions most frequently asked by many Indian aspirants.

HEC PARIS

Interview with Mr. Philippe Oster, Director of Communications, Development and Admissions

Why does the average GMAT score for Indians tend to be higher?

The average GMAT score tends to be higher amongst our Indian candidates and this due to certain hallmarks of the Indian education system which lead their students to GMAT success. For example, it is a competitive environment where education is highly valued. Further to this it is a country in which a good business education is considered valuable, and the MBA is a widely recognized degree — this is a motivating factor for Indian applicants. A particularly important point is that India favors assessment formats that prepare potential MBA candidates for the format of the GMAT test, namely multiple choice evaluations.

Despite a diverse profile and fantastic work experience, do candidates with lower than average GMAT scores tend to get sidelined over higher scores?

It is important to state that the minimum GMAT score of 600 is a prerequisite for HEC Paris MBA. We have to be ensured that the candidate has the intellectual agility to fully participate in classes given on subject matters with which they might not be familiar, and a high GMAT score is a good indicator of this. However, that being said, a lower GMAT score can be somewhat mitigated by having exceptional work experience, which can indeed make a difference to the candidate's application status. For the sake of reference, the average GMAT score for our Indian applicants is 705, the median is 700, and the mid 80% range falls between 670 and 770.

After 3–4 years of domestic experience, not much of which is managerial, and no international experience, aspirants are afraid that they'll fall short, even despite showing potential. What really qualifies as quality work experience?

Frankly speaking, candidates with three years of non-managerial, non-international work experience should probably reconsider their application. Our MBA applicants have on an average six years of work experience, the majority of which is managerial, and also have a good deal of international exposure. It should be noted that international exposure can be procured by working overseas, or personal travel, and also by working domestically in an international team, or working with international clients.

How relevant is an aspirant's job profile in their post-MBA job hunt?

A candidate's pre-MBA profile plays a significant role in their ensuing job hunt post-MBA. Employers need to know that a candidate has a history of consistent achievement and success, and that there is a clear line of progression in their career timeline. Previous work achievements demonstrate potential, and could therefore swing the odds in a candidate's favor.

What are the risks and opportunities for someone who wants to change industry or function?

All MBA candidates we see want to change function in some way, whether it's progressing upwards in a similar role, or wanting to work in a different capacity in the same industry. Switching industry, geographical locations, or working language, however, are all slightly more challenging, especially if the student in question wants to change more than one of these aspects of their career. The problem faced by a lot of other MBA programs is that they are simply too short to allow for this level of change. However, at HEC Paris, MBA participants can study and work for up to 16 months, including undertaking fieldwork projects or internships with companies in their target industry, location, or even language. This flexibility and time allows our students to put the necessary measures in place to drastically transform their career—whether that means taking a particular specialization, or securing relevant work experience.

Many aspirants come from the STEM background and the line connecting the present to the future is more than gray. Quite frankly, most are career changers are looking for a new academic challenge in the management discipline, with not much idea of what they want to do post-MBA. How can these aspirants present their cases from a position of strength?

Our students can be best split into two categories—the hunters, and the explorers. The former come to the campus with a very clear idea of what they want to do post-MBA, and want to be "fast-tracked" as quickly as possible. There are, on the other hand, a large number of the latter, who do not have a clear target, and who are considering a number of options. Not having a clear idea in mind of what they want to post-MBA is not a deterring factor from an admissions standpoint, as long as the candidate demonstrates interest, potential, and a genuine willingness to learn.

What are some of the transferrable skills from one industry to another?

While the target industries of our MBA participants vary widely, there are common skills between them, which have made the transition between industries easier for the industry-switchers in the programme. For example, those from STEM backgrounds are usually well-equipped with an analytic mindset and a wealth of product knowledge that could benefit them in industries such as marketing and consulting. The ability to lead and work in a team transcends industry barriers, and is usually considered one of the most important skills to possess by a huge range of industries.

Additionally, given that 90% of the HEC Paris MBA students are international and hail from over 50 countries, there is no short supply of bilingual and multilingual candidates. With the business world more globalized than ever before, the ability to speak multiple languages will also set students in good stride for switching industry.

Does HEC Paris accept aspirants who already have an MBA from an Indian institute? If yes, are there any additional screening criteria for them?

Yes, we do accept candidates who have previously undertaken an MBA from an Indian institute, but we will challenge them during the recruitment process in order to understand their motivation in doing so. There will be no additional screening criteria, but they should be prepared to give a clear explanation of their rationale, as well as demonstrate a clear progression of work experience following their first MBA.

ESADE Business School

Interview with Ms. Mary Granger, Regional Director, Asia

Why does the average GMAT score for Indians tend to be higher?

Because traditionally, strong students in India are encouraged to enter Engineering programs, this tends to improve already strong quantitative backgrounds, making their GMAT scores very competitive. Also, even in non-Engineering programs, we have heard from students that the majority of high schools and university-level programs in India base their grades on quantitative exams, so the majority of students are used to the kind of test structure given by the GMAT, compared to students coming from other regions.

In addition, the large volume of Indian candidates means that they often retake the GMAT test (even if they have already scored 700+) to try to stand out based on this score, whereas in some other countries, they only take the GMAT once or perhaps twice. I believe that there is a perception on the part of many Indian candidates that the admissions decisions are based mostly on the GMAT score, so they focus on this as being one of the easier aspects to improve in the short-term. However, this is only one part of the admission decision, and we try to focus on the whole profile.

Despite a diverse profile and fantastic work experience, do candidates with lower than average GMAT scores tend to get sidelined over high scorers?

At ESADE this isn't the case, as we look at the holistic profile of the candidate. We are looking for great communicators, not only great number crunchers. There are two reasons for our doing this:

- On one hand, well-rounded candidates tend to add more to class discussions and also work better on teams. Since ESADE is so team-focused, we value these skills.
- Secondly, when we speak with companies, they never say they are looking for number-crunchers. While strong quant and analytic skills are certainly valuable to companies, the skills they most seek are communication skills, teamwork skills, leadership skills — all of which are things we try to target in admissions.
- Lastly, we usually mention to the candidates that we require submission of GMAT test scores, not because there is a minimum cut off line at Admissions, but because it is one component to evaluate their level of preparation to do an MBA and their capacity to be able to follow our demanding MBA classes comfortably.

After 3–4 years of domestic experience, not much of which is managerial, and no international experience, aspirants are afraid that they'll fall short, even despite showing potential. What really qualifies as quality work experience?

Tell us your story! We want to know how you made a positive impact in your work environment (Increasing sales? Decreasing error? Motivating teammates? Providing innovative solutions to complex problems? Etc.). We would like to know how and why you make decisions in the your professional career. Have you taken deliberate steps to develop your skills? We don't specifically target candidates without managerial and/or international experience, but certainly candidates without this background can take part in the MBA if they show they learn from their mistakes, strive for improvement, and initiate changes in their organizations. If an Indian candidate can transcend India's borders, despite not having international experience, we are open to their joining ESADE.

Also, by "international experience" we are looking at both elements: 1. Physically have been outside of India, meaning have traveled, lived, studied or worked abroad and 2. Have they extensively worked in international teams involving global clients, partners or colleagues in other countries. Most of our students come with both elements, but if not, it is important to elaborate on what kind of international interactions they have had.

How relevant is an aspirant's job profile in their post-MBA job hunt?

The aspirant's job profile is extremely relevant. Companies are looking for "transferable skills" which can be used in their organizations. It is extremely challenging to make a "triple jump" (functional area, industry, geography), and it's risky for companies to bet on someone trying to do this, so they often try to find aspects of an aspirant's previous experience which will transfer directly. If someone does want to make a big shift, we would encourage them to take advantage of the additional aspects of the MBA, such as Labs, Clubs, internships, Action Learning Consulting Projects, Case Competitions – all of which can help shore up a profile which may be lacking directly transferable skills. The internship will definitely play an important role to make a career change, not only as it will show the recruiters that the candidate has had some experience in the new field they want to jump in, but also for the candidate to make sure that this is the change they want to make post-MBA.

What are the risks and opportunities for someone who wants to change industry or function?

Generally, the more changes, the more of a challenge this represents, both for the candidate (who may be lacking some essential skills for the new position) and also for the company (which will invest time and energy in training which may not be successful). On the other hand, we have clear examples of successful students who have leveraged opportunities on campus to make the changes they were seeking, including the "triple jump." So it is possible but it would be challenging.

Many aspirants come from the STEM background and the line connecting the present to the future is more than gray. Quite frankly, most are career changers and are looking for a new academic challenge in the management discipline, with not much idea of what they want post-MBA. How can these aspirants present their cases from a position of strength?

I think we expect these candidates to be very inquisitive, looking for "something more" than a technical role, and they should also couple this striving with strong communication and leadership skills. They should focus less on their technical skills in the essays and the interview (as well as their CV), as the roles they will seek post-MBA will not be based on these skills. They need to realize that the person interviewing them (for admission to the MBA, or for the post-MBA job) may not have a technical background, so they need to be able to articulate their relevant skills and how they will add value to the organization.

What are some of the transferable skills from one industry to another?

Communication is key — being able to communicate between people with different backgrounds, which is the environment they will find in their post-MBA career. It is also important to be able to communicate vision to a team. Leadership, flexibility and teamwork are also key skills which are important to transfer to the new career.

Does ESADE accept aspirants who already have an MBA from an Indian institute? If yes, are there any additional screening criteria for them?

We have, on occasions, done so. This means that having done an MBA from an Indian institute is not an automatic disqualifier, but the candidate must be prepared to explain the reasoning behind wanting to do a second MBA, and must realize that it is an exceptional situation and he or she will be asked about this decision not only during the admissions process, but also in their future job interviews.

And lastly, what particularly is ESADE looking for in an Indian aspirant?

We look at the Indian candidates as we look at the rest of our cohort—we try to be coherent and not differentiate between nationalities, because we feel that the ideal candidate should be a global citizen, able to work in multinational and multifunctional teams, while bringing value to the cohort by sharing his or her previous experience and cultural insights.

Please add anything else that you'd like to give as advice to the Indian applicant.

Please be honest in your essays and interview. One reason for the interview itself is to evaluate if we are able to help you meet your professional aspirations through the program, and if you aren't honest with your objectives, you may be disappointed with the results, and you could have avoided that disappointment.

In addition, try to research as much as possible about ESADE, by visiting the campus, or attending a class, meeting with students or alumni in person or via email, so that you can decide if we are the right fit for you. Few of our Indian candidates come to visit, but we feel that visiting the campus and getting to know us better is one of the best things candidates can do to stand out and also to help them understand our culture. If not, we encourage students to come to one of the local events we conduct in India, for example the information sessions, to get an insight of ESADE.

Don't rely only on rankings to choose your target schools and make your final decision. At the end of the day you will have many professional opportunities in the long-term post-MBA, so try to choose the program which is best for your long-term aspirations, and also gives you the best possible MBA experience.

HKUST

Interview with Mr. Gary Lo, Head of Marketing and Admissions

Why does the average GMAT score for Indians tend to be higher?

The candidates tend to be more competitive hence GMAT scores are higher, in general, from India.

Despite a diverse profile and fantastic work experience, do candidates with lower than average GMAT scores tend to get sidelined over high scorers?

Really, it depends on the overall profile. Personality, communication skills and cultural fit will also be key criteria for assessment.

After 3–4 years of domestic experience, not much of which is managerial, and no international experience, aspirants are afraid that they'll fall short, even despite showing potential. What really qualifies as quality work experience?

Large corporates, MNC, and international experience or assignment will definitely be a plus. We will also look into key achievements in candidates' career to see if they are result-oriented.

How relevant is an aspirant's job profile in their post-MBA job hunt?

Highly relevant, as employers will screen through CVs with the same eye.

What are the risks and opportunities for someone who wants to change industry or function?

Opportunities are — definitely a life transformation experience, doing something you enjoy and hopefully with a great package. Risks are — you will be competing with other candidates who might have prior experience in that particular industry, and you would need to build a strong case why you stand out. Having a plan B or being flexible will always be helpful in the process.

Many aspirants come from the STEM background and the line connecting the present to the future is more than gray. Quite frankly, most are career changers and are looking for a new academic challenge in the management discipline, with not much idea of what they want post-MBA. How can these aspirants present their cases from a position of strength?

It is advised they get more opinion from alumni or seniors on potential paths after the MBA, and also explore the pros and cons. With a clear goal during the MBA, it would be much easier to focus on the right resources and connections that you need. Time is limited here and the earlier you find your focus, the more likely you can benefit more.

What are some of the transferable skills from one industry to another?

Communication skills, interpersonal skills, project management skills.

Does HKUST accept aspirants who already have an MBA from an Indian institute. If yes, are there any additional screening criteria for them?

No additional screening, but we would need a strong case for why they feel the second MBA can be beneficial for them.

What particularly is HKUST looking for in an Indian aspirant?

It is the same as candidates from other nationalities — we look at academic history, test scores, working background, career goals and cultural fit.

Georgetown McDonough

Interview with Ms. Shari Hubert, Associate Dean of Admissions

The Georgetown experience

Our MBA program's goal is to transform our students into principled leaders, who will have an impact on both business and society. While we focus on core courses and electives across a wide range of areas, we also make sure that our students understand the global economy. Our introductory course on the Structure of Global Industries teaches team dynamics, communication skills, and the dynamics of global markets. We also offer the Global Business Experience, a live international consulting opportunity that gives students an opportunity to apply what they have learned.

Our career fairs and career services office support students to find jobs where their geographical preferences lie. Our international students receive an industry/functional coach as well as an international coach, who helps them navigate the H1-B process. On a one-on-one basis, we definitely have students who find global employment, but this depends on finding the right opportunities as well. Some students are able to get into a global organization in the U.S., and then travel internally to other geographies. On the other hand, we also have some of our international graduates who prefer to work in the U.S. I won't proclaim that it is easy to find US jobs if you need sponsorship, but we have had students who were successful. They tended to work hard at doing their homework, understanding the needs of the organization and being well versed in telling their story and how their background, experience and skills related to the position at hand. Overall, 91% of our FT graduates find employment within 3 months of graduation. We also have a great entrepreneurship initiative for students from a family business background.

About work experience and overall profile
We like to see our applicants as well-rounded people, irrespective of the industry that they come from. We understand that many Indian candidates come from highly technical backgrounds rather than business. The technical skills are a plus in their ability to handle the rigor of the program, but what we want them to do is to demonstrate the impact they have had in their organizations with their skills. Have they shown leadership? Have they managed teams? In what ways have they impacted their business units and their organizations, beyond the technical? STEM candidates, like candidates from other backgrounds, are judged based on their achievements, impact, and overall profile. DC is becoming quite the technology hub, so there tends to be opportunities for individuals with technical backgrounds with an MBA.

There is no minimum experience required, but the average is 4–5 years, though what is more important than the quantity is definitely the quality. Strong applicants are able to demonstrate why their experience is important and what they have done and achieved, rather than merely show that they've been busy in a job. Also, it's important that applicants from other countries have a clear understanding and appreciation for US cultural and professional norms in business and in business school. Those who have either worked, lived or studied abroad may have a competitive advantage and an easier time adapting.

When to apply
We have three rounds—in October, January and March. Applying in an earlier round increases the chances of getting a scholarship, given that funds can be limited as time goes on. It also allows more time to process an admitted student's visa. For international students, we recommend applying in either the first or second rounds. All our scholarships are merit-based only and there is no need to apply separately.

Our graduates learn skills that go beyond only what they would apply in a job. We are strong on providing a general management education. We are strong on inculcating global perspectives. We are strong in inculcating ethical decision making. We want to offer our students a transformative experience. Our career services office is effective and excellent. We offer an excellent learning environment that helps students to achieve their career aims, no matter what background they come from, as long as they are willing to put in the hard work and effort as well.

About second MBAs

In terms of whether we accept individuals who already have an MBA. The answer is, "it depends." They are not ineligible to apply, but we look carefully at their rationale to determine what additional benefit they would gain by receiving a second MBA. I would say that it is rare that these candidates are accepted. Chances are higher if it's only a one year MBA that they may have pursued initially. With that said, we love to see applicants with Master's degrees in disciplines other than business.

Simon Business School, University of Rochester

Interview with Rebekah Lewin, Assistant Dean for Admissions and Student Engagement

Why does the average GMAT score for Indians tend to be higher?

Many Indian candidates have strong technical training in Engineering and Math. That helps with the quantitative portion of the GMAT.

Despite a diverse profile and fantastic work experience, do candidates with lower than average GMAT scores tend to get sidelined over high scorers?

At Rochester, we will take a holistic approach when looking at candidates. However, if a candidate has significantly lower scores, there may be concerns about their capabilities to succeed in our academically rigorous program. A diverse profile and fantastic work experience is really important, so I would suggest speaking with Admissions Officers at target schools for more feedback.

After 3–4 years of domestic experience, not much of which is managerial, and no international experience, aspirants are afraid that they'll fall short, even despite showing potential. What really qualifies as quality work experience?

We are looking at the years of cumulative work experience, growth within that period of time — in terms of promotions and increasing responsibility — as well as performance. We'd love to see experience leading a project or a team in the workplace, and we do not require that a student has been a manager prior to B-School.

How relevant is an aspirant's job profile in their post-MBA job hunt?

It is really important as it helps us to determine if the student is a fit for our program and typical career opportunities available. We take feedback from our Career Management Center and their conversations with Corporate Recruiters when we review candidates in Admissions Committee. This helps us to confirm that we can meet a student's expectations and that they have been introspective about their reasons for the MBA and how it fits into their career development.

Does Simon accept aspirants who already have an MBA from an Indian institute? If yes, are there any additional screening criteria for them?

Yes, we will accept candidates with a prior MBA. We are looking for candidates to make the case of why the second MBA and to make sure there is a career fit — but this is similar to our screening of all candidates.

And lastly, what particularly is Simon looking for in an Indian aspirant?

Strong communication skills, a combination of motivation/drive and humility, ability to adapt to different situations and environments — ideally with cross cultural exposure. Most enrolling students have between 3 to 8 years of full-time experience and well-developed career goals that fit one of our three main areas of post-MBA job opportunities — finance, quantitative marketing or consulting.

IE Business School, Spain

Giada Maria Rapisarda, Admissions Assistant at IE Business School

About common weak areas observed in Indian applicants

In general, I would like to say that Indian candidates are not less prepared than others, that's why it is difficult to say which lacunae they can have. Therefore, I have found some points that are general and, of course, don't affect all Indian profiles. So, from my experience I would say that their weakness could be:

1) Lack of international experience: We always look for diversity and for international profiles. Some Indian candidates have professional experience related only to their country.

2) Indian culture is deeply related with social and professional hierarchy, therefore sometimes Indian candidates, during the admissions process, give a lot of importance if they are talking to the Director of the program or to the assistant.

3) Indian candidates sometimes have low academic transcripts.

These are the main aspects I would underline. However, I want to say that we had lots of brilliant Indian candidates and I see them as very interesting and brilliant.

MISB Bocconi

Interview with Mr. Alessandro Giuliani, Managing Director

Why does the average GMAT score for Indians tend to be higher?

Indians are considered to be very strong academically across the globe. Specifically, Indians are very good in quantitative and logical reasoning. English is taught at various levels at most of the schools from the very beginning. Because of these factors, Indians tend to have a higher GMAT score.

Despite a diverse profile and fantastic work experience, do candidates with lower than average GMAT scores tend to get sidelined over higher scores?

This used to be the case, but I think schools across the globe understand the advantages of an overall, well rounded profile than the ones that just have high scores. Various schools have detailed, essay type of questions as part of their application, which enables them to understand the thought process, analytical abilities, leadership skills, etc., in an applicant.

So, the key is preparing your application dossier for colleges, highlighting all the aspects such as extra-curricular activities, referrals, special achievements in the academic level and at the professional level. The ability to put across well thought out answers and story will give an edge to the students who might have average scores, but very strong profiles. So, a higher GMAT score is not the only criterion for selection—it is the overall profile of the student.

After 3–4 years of domestic experience, not much of which is managerial, and no international experience, aspirants are afraid that they'll fall short, even despite showing potential. What really qualifies as quality work experience? Does MISB accept candidates with lower than average work experience?

Any work experience brings its own added value.

An experienced student brings in many attributes to the class, such as teamwork, team understanding of a corporate environment, hands-on work experience, ability to work with different individuals, structured thought process, etc., which improve class participation. On the other side, freshers are students who do not have any prior baggage and are very easily molded and more open to learning, as they are just starting on their journey of experiences.

At MISB, we try to have a well distributed percentage for both these categories and the PGPB, our flagship program, is specifically designed for Freshers and Young professionals.

How relevant is an aspirant's job profile in their post-MBA job hunt?

Some companies clearly ask for job experience, and in that case same sector experience plays a crucial role in the selection. Other companies prefer no work-ex at all. So it varies from company to company.

What have MISB's placements been like?

MISB Bocconi has had two batches that have graduated with 100% placements and exciting job profiles.

Bocconi, being ranked 7th worldwide in Business courses by QS Rankings, most MNCs and big Indian companies know MISB Bocconi. Our students are selected through a very effective process of admission and selection and then go through a very exhaustive and intense academic experience. Their strong global exposure helps in differentiating them from other B-School students. Also, our students are considered industry ready by recruiters.

What are the risks and opportunities for someone who wants to change industry or function?

A change in industry or function can be justified by the intent behind the change. There are always tradeoffs between risks and opportunities while changing an industry or function.

The risks could be: the previous work experience might not be too relevant, drop in remuneration, time investment in learning new things from scratch, amongst others.

Tentative opportunities could be: learning a new skill-set in an ever changing environment, expanding professional horizons, discovering own capabilities, building adaptability across functions or industries

Ideally, before switching, it is advised that one must make a risk and opportunity assessment plan, as well as take stock of the motivation behind the switch.

What are some transferable skills from one industry to the other?

There are different skill-sets needed for different industries, but there are always some skills which acts as a strong foundation for any industry. Managing a team, leadership style, analytical skills, verbal and written communication, research abilities, are a few of them.

SAMPLE ESSAYS

- GOALS
- DIVERSITY AND CONTRIBUTION
- TELL US ABOUT YOURSELF
- ACHIEVEMENTS
- CHALLENGES
- STRENGTHS AND WEAKNESSES
- LEADERSHIP AND TEAM SKILLS

Goals

The goals essay is the most important component of your applications. It is the fundamental building block around which your other complementary essays will be built. You cannot afford to get this wrong. Business schools see whether you want an MBA just for the prestige of it or you genuinely have your head on your shoulders, are mature enough to make your career choices and how the school fits into them. This is not the place to try your creative ideas but rather one where you capture the Admissions Committee's interest, to retain it and enthuse them enough to call you for an interview.

Most schools will ask you to define your short-term and long-term goals. Really, there is no right or wrong approach to tackle this one, just a perfect personal statement, totally relevant to you, is needed. Before you go ahead and answer this vital question, consider these important phases of your life:

- How has your career so far prepared you for business school? How has it led you to conclude that an MBA is the stepping stone to your future career aspirations?
- Why is now the best time to do an MBA?
- What knowledge and skills do you hope to gain from the degree which will help your career move in the direction you envision?
- What are your goals and how will an MBA help you achieve them?

Most goals essays have a common theme. They are about logically stringing together your career aspirations with how your career so far has prepared you for them. Also, are you qualified to achieve these goals, with the help of management education? What you need to do is reflect, think and make a holistic argument justifying the need for an MBA and how you will achieve your goals through it.

1. What are your short-term career plans immediately post-MBA, and why is an Ivey MBA essential to those plans? (250 word limit)

I want to design a career that combines my interest in Operations Management and diverse professional exposure to the manufacturing industry. Leveraging my Ivey MBA and experience of working with cross functional teams across different countries, I now want to transition from a technical role to a managerial one.

At Bridgestone, I have utilized and analyzed prevailing quality issues and conducted process capability studies using statistical tools. I have met quality and efficiency targets by closely working with teams from planning, production, maintenance and engineering departments. Having recognized my flair for process optimization and honed my technical and people skills, now is the right time for me to broaden my knowledge base to be exposed to better career opportunities.

Immediately after my Ivey MBA, I want to work with a company like 3M, SABIC or Nestle, playing an instrumental role in its smooth operations. Long-term, I see myself progressing to a senior management position wherein I can be a key stakeholder in decision making processes and contribute to my organization's growth, profitability and success.

Ivey is my top choice for many reasons, the first one being its location. My family is in Toronto and I want to work and live in Canada, post MBA. Apart from a dynamic evolving curriculum, Ivey boasts of an excellent pool of faculty and a truly diverse student body, whose experiences I will be able to draw learning from, while sharing my own experiences to make learning more interactive and enriching for each one involved.

2. How does the ISB PGP tie-in with your career goals? (300 words max.)

At headline level, I foresee myself as a top business leader propelling, developing and inspiring diverse teams, in the energy sector.

As a civil engineer in the government sector with NTPC, I am privy to on-field, operational and technical insights. Rubbing shoulders with senior managers and contractors has triggered an immense interest in understanding the business side of my job. An MBA will unite my technical knowledge, skills and expertise with current business practices, seamlessly.

Post MBA, I intend to join a large energy sector company like URS Corporation and utilize my structured business knowledge to efficiently manage mega projects and drive them to completion, overcoming all challenges. Leveraging my past experience and newly learnt skills, I see myself working with a major energy establishment as the Project Manager of an independent project. In the long run, I see myself in the driver's seat, as an important component of upper management and navigating my organization successfully for sustained growth.

ISB, with its emphasis on global business awareness, team based learning and a versatile curriculum, would be a perfect vehicle for me to understand the current business environment. Having worked in the government sector, I wish to gain insights of the private sector and what better way to do so than by sharing experiences and viewpoints from eminently diverse cohorts! Programs like Operations Management, LEAD, etc., are exactly what I am looking for to enhance my skill set. Financial courses like Corporate Control and Financial Engineering will help me understand the monetary implications while handling significant projects in the future. By networking with like-minded peers at the General Management Club and the Energy Club, I wish to expand the horizons of my learning.

ISB will catapult my career radically and with its excellent brand value, give me top opportunities. Its holistic education will be a wholesome experience for my well-rounded growth.

3. **We find that students apply to our programs for a variety of personal and professional reasons. What do you hope to gain from the Duke MBA and how will it support you in your personal and professional goals? If you are interested in a specific concentration or the HSM Certificate, please discuss in this essay. (1.5 line spacing, two pages, font more than 10)**

The Duke MBA program is a natural extension of my professional pursuits over the last five years. Professionally, it is one of the few programs designed to expand my knowledge on global business with the stress on Energy and Environment, while continuing my growth in leadership roles within Cameron. On a personal level, I see the program as the ideal bridge connecting my technical knowledge and my global background with superior management education from Duke, which will help me improve my company's landscape socially, environmentally and financially.

The *Oil and Gas* sector exhibits its own inherent risks (Exxon Valdez, Macondo, Burma Agate, Megaborg, etc.) and demands a robust Sustainable Enterprise system. Through the Duke MBA program, with a concentration in *Energy and Environment*, I want to bring about sweeping changes and successfully implement Sustainable Supply Chain programs within Cameron. Also, by working actively on upstream supply chain continuous improvement projects, I want to educate our suppliers (spread across the globe) to reduce carbon emissions logistically and adopt the best industry standards (sustainability targets, end customer expectations, legal requirements, etc.). The path to a Sustainable Enterprise is at its infancy and I am in a position within the company where I can drive this change, top-down. Eventually, I hope to grow to an Executive position where I have a role to play in my organization's overall operations, growth and success.

Goals

To describe my career at Cameron, I started in a two-year Management Training program, with consecutive six-month rotations. Within the first rotation, I was noted for my strong leadership potential. I was commended for managing the Oklahoma City facility expansion project, while concurrently handling multiple capital improvement projects and attaining my Six Sigma Green Belt Certification. Incidentally, I was the only employee in the history of the organization to have achieved three major industry certifications during the two-year rotation programme.

Subsequently, I managed a warehouse with 13 direct reports and was responsible for over $13 million of inventory. Next, deployed at Division Corporate, I got exposure to strategic projects and created financial business models to assess inventory risk and returns at our Global Aftermarket locations. On the final rotation, again at Division Corporate, I analyzed Global Supply Chain spend, as it related to the company's bottom line, and presented recommendations to the Executive team.

I was the top candidate out of the Management Training program and rose quickly in my position as a Global Supply Chain Specialist. Starting off with a portfolio spend of $30 million, I gradually worked on larger portfolios. In little more than a year, I was managing a Regional Sourcing team out of India.

It was during this time that I got my first exposure to Green Supply Chain initiatives, where I observed some suppliers using Vapor Corrosion Inhibitors (VCI) for all their packaging. After that, I worked with my team to switch all suppliers to VCI packaging and eliminate using oil pollutants. Within a year of managing a $70 million portfolio of Regional Sourcing Team and local commodities, I was promoted to Corporate Shared Services to help design Global Business Strategies for the $1.2 billion Indirect Procurement and Logistics business.

Although I am excited with my success at the firm, this is an opportune time for me to get a strong yet flexible management education grounding to add more value to Cameron, making it more strong and resilient. I believe the MBA program at Duke University, combined with my work experience, is my path to attain this goal. In short, I need Duke's cross cultural program to learn more, be more and do more.

While many MBA programs will increase my functional competence and develop business specific aptitudes, Duke fits my aspirations to a T. With my research and my interactions with Jessica at the Admissions Office, I have become keenly aware of Duke's commitment to innovation, globalism and path breaking teaching methodology. By interacting with a student body from various industries and understanding legal requirements, I look forward to setting key benchmarks for Environmental, Health and Safety and Social/Economic standards. I am convinced that Duke's commitment to the students, and the business community at large, is the foundation of a truly unique and rewarding educational experience.

Ultimately, I am confident that my professional experience and my intellectual hunger have prepared me well for the Duke MBA experience. I am positive that getting a strong education in the management fundamentals, with specialization in *Energy and Environment*, will make me a wiser leader and more effective change agent for my organization.

4. What will your future look like after completing your MBA? (500 words)

At Goodyear, I underwent basic orientation in business processes, along with several management courses at the rubber mixing plant at Beaumont, Texas USA. Here, I completed an extremely challenging project in which I increased the efficiency of an existing, outdated system. Due to this success, I was called to the US again last year for a second project to improve efficiency and to Thailand, to solve an ergonomics issue, where I delivered 400% results. To prepare me for my current BUL (Business Unit Leader) role at Aurangabad, I also trained as BUL in Group 6 at Gadsden, Alabama.

These multicultural and cross functional experiences, spanning three different continents, have been extremely gratifying and whetted my desire to explore Management Consulting further. I find the field extremely challenging, dynamic and interesting. Post MBA, I want to join a top Strategic Consulting firm, such as McKinsey and Bain, where I can get a ground level experience of offering solutions that are innovative, yet easy to execute and can integrate strategy with implementation to fetch outstanding results. While gaining this broad, holistic experience, I anticipate working with high profile clients and to position myself to meet high customer expectations. Eventually, I would like to become an integral part of the decision making processes and pitch myself for senior management responsibilities in my organization.

By that time, I should, ideally, have gained sufficient expertise in all areas such as procurement, logistics, sales and distribution, to head a consulting department efficiently. I will be able to effectively leverage my excellent interpersonal and managerial skills to lead teams of highly motivated and skilled individuals to deliver quality services, which will optimize business opportunities for my clients and give them excellent "Return on Investments". With a 360 degree view of the industry, combined with my drive and initiative, I hope to establish myself firmly and keep my company a step ahead in the vigorously competitive market.

London Business School is the right place to complement my experience and goals, primarily due to its excellent brand value, which can accelerate my pace of growth. As a future consultant, I need to hone my skills of assimilating information and taking critical decisions. I also need to further develop my leadership style to motivate diverse work groups and negotiate effectively. I hope to acquire these at LBS, since group studies form an important part of the MBA programme.

Despite having international experience, I am not very aware of the major markets of several under-represented countries. Diversity being a key feature of LBS, working shoulder to shoulder with international members who are driven with their distinctive set of strengths and talents, will give me the required insights and refine my knowledge and skills. The flexible curriculum will allow me to charter my own career trajectory and I am excited about choosing from 70 different electives.

Attending LBS will enable me build upon my leadership skills that will be crucial throughout my future.

5. How does the ISB PGP tie-in with your career goals? (300 words max)

I have worked as an Analyst and then as an Associate Consultant with Deloitte and Ernst and Young respectively. While the former offered incomparable learning potential and exposure to the dynamic work culture of a consulting organization, the latter left me unfulfilled and dissatisfied. My work was limited to copying and pasting using MS Office and cold calling on leads. Despite being fully aware that I would grow there with time, I decided to quit.

At that time, I approached Arpana Group of Trusts, an NGO with which I have been associated since college. Their school provides outside class tuition support to 1,500 slum children. When I discussed my professional predicament with them, I was immediately offered full time employment. Here, I help raise funds and counsel students, and also assist in placing the graduating students at relevant jobs suited to their career interests and skills.

Spending countless hours attending late night calls, monitoring progress and counseling marginalized children, led me to discover such projects' phenomenal impact and outreach. In one such project, we prepared CDs according to grade level curriculum and distributed them at schools. Working, learning and growing in my social responsibilities, as well as discussing my aspirations, have helped me identify my goals.

Upon graduating from ISB, I aspire to take up a Consulting role in a for-profit capacity, serving the nonprofit sector. Organizations like Dasra or Ashoka will be good fits, where I can establish public-private-nonprofit partnerships. Long-term, I intend to establish a consultancy that serves and empowers non-profit organizations to achieve their social and operational goals.

ISB, with its strong consulting focus, excellent brand value and location (I want to work and live in India), is a natural choice and I apply with it being my next step towards the fulfillment of my professional and personal goals.

6. How do you hope to see your career developing over the next 5 years? How will the MBA and Oxford assist you in the development of these ambitions? (500 words)

"You're crazy!" that's what my colleagues and friends said when I told them I planned to quit my job as a Business Analyst. Here I am, with 10 years of solid professional experience managing and developing products for US banks and financial institutions. I am at the cusp of transitioning into senior roles with higher responsibilities. And I want to quit and pursue my passion—starting India's first international Ultra Marathon Company, which will regularly organize events in diverse terrains around the world.

As a new company, entering a totally untapped market, I will need all the elements on my side. My response to my friends was, "I'll learn how business is done from the best, then I'll go ahead and do it!" So, here I am, knocking on Said Business School's doors, with a burning desire to learn all about entrepreneurship—right from starting a venture, to making it profitable.

I have been running marathons almost as long as I have been working professionally. In a documentary film (link attached under essay), in which I was featured, I was called a woman who prevails through the unexpected. Despite being the first Indian woman who completed a 135 mile run on altitudes as high as 18,000 feet, I feel humbled and disappointed that the management of running events in India is below standards as compared to other parts of the world.

Many aspiring marathon runners get dejected right after the first run, because of lack of basic infrastructure like no of water at regular intervals, no finish mats and no medical infrastructure in case of emergencies. There's no company functioning as per international standards and meeting the basic requirements. I want to bridge this gap. Over the long-term, I want to dedicate my time and efforts to generating employment in rural areas and concentrate my efforts towards creating opportunities and avenues for development of the girl child in India, specifically my own State, which sadly has the highest illiteracy rate for girls.

However, there are certain pieces missing before I can acutally realize this vision. I need an outstanding curriculum that assimilates and reconciles my ambitions — one that teaches me about planning, resource allocation, marketing, budgeting, selling and networking, so as to get cracking on my nascent idea. A Said MBA will assist me in obtaining skills needed for successful entrepreneurship and management. While in the programme, I want to focus on Entrepreneurship related concentrations like *Global Strategy*, *Entrepreneurial Finance* and *Delivering Infrastructure Cheaper and faster;* they speak directly to my goals. *Corporate Valuation* and *Reputation and Leadership* will allow me to get intrinsic insights into bottlenecks which small scale start-up business face, so that I can arrest them in time.

I look forward to collaborating with and learning from a truly multicultural community of students and acquiring the latest industry insights through the cutting edge industry specific curriculum. With all that it offers, I apply unabashedly to SAID, with it being my top choice MBA.

7. **UCLA Anderson is distinguished by three defining principles: Share Success, Think Fearlessly, Drive Change. What principles have defined your life and pre-MBA career? How do you believe that UCLA Anderson's principles, and the environment they create, will help you attain your post-MBA career goals? (750 words maximum)**

"Porashona kore je gaadi ghoda chore she." This is a Bengali phrase that means "Those who study hard are the ones who see the world." This is the first lesson about education that Bengali parents impart to their children. My parents, too, pinned their highest hopes on my academic credentials. Since childhood, my life revolved around this singularity of "excellence", an important principle of my life.

While studying at Jadavpur University, one of the top tier technical institutes in India, I was touched by the history behind the institution. It was founded by a handful of social leaders of the pre-independence era, with a vision of educating India's youth in various disciplines of technology to make India an intellectually independent nation. The idea of an independent spirit resonated with my ideologies. The value system of the Tata Group has only strengthened this ideology since.

Here, at Tata Steel, I have endeavored to stretch myself beyond defined boundaries, test limits and explore possibilities. During my traineeship period, I innovated on a new process to galvanize hollow tubes called Galnext. It just received a patent last month. In 2013, when I was the on-site manager for two separate mechanical installations, I noticed that the project schedule did not consider the oncoming monsoons, which could delay it by two months. The water could not be banked at ground level; it would cause stagnation and hamper one team's work. If we allowed it to flow over the side-walls to the basement, the second team could not continue their welding job. I suggested making a concrete bank with a single opening that could be shifted as needed.

It would let the water flow without soaking everything and the plate-welding could continue. Although appreciated, my idea was challenged. "The 'extra' work would need teams to share resources and would lead to planning and billing complexities". If I wanted to go ahead, I needed to shoulder the full responsibility. I did, and my calculated risk paid off. When implemented on-site, the idea resulted in an increased rate of progress and cost-savings due to reduced idle time, as the project delay was brought down to just about twenty days.

Today, I feel proud to have made such tangible contributions to my organization. While I have leveraged my analytical and technical skills to drive change through various projects that I have undertaken, I have also realized that my work is only a part of the big picture. As I aspire to transition into Operations Management, the need to shore up again on my education cannot be overstated.

I want to understand factors that drive policy changes and affect processes. I want to learn how to assess quality, manage inventory and understand the role that technology can play in streamlining operations. Acquiring strong management grounding will help me understand all components of an enterprise, their strengths and inter-dependencies. Only then I can be a more effective catalyst for positive change in my organization by reducing bottlenecks and improving system efficiency, while sustaining quality.

An MBA from UCLA Anderson will be the ideal way to get started. The school's principles promise me an exhilarating environment, one in which I can thrive, grow and train to become a dynamic leader who can quickly adapt to the business world. The Anderson strategic plan 2016 shows the school's commitment towards its students and I am bound to benefit from joining at such an opportune time. With the truly flexible curriculum, I will get to charter my own study path, based on my goals, right from the time I join. Additionally, specialized tracks will provide the depth of knowledge I seek.

I was particularly excited to find out more about the Automotive Business Association, which will provide me a chance to explore a possible Operations role in the automotive industry. It will be most exciting to convert my passion for the automobile industry into a career!

The Applied Management Research will help me put whatever I learn in the classroom to practice by working on a real-world problem and develop business models along the way. Also, with its courses designed to develop analytical skills, practise managerial communication and be adept at leading both small and large teams, a host of courses will provide the depth required to master the ideas regarding the science of operations. With its principles of thinking fearlessly, sharing success and driving change, the institution exemplifies some of my own driving forces in life. No wonder, it's my top choice study destination.

Goals

8. Please provide a personal statement. It should not exceed 500 words and must include the following: What are your short-term and long-term career objectives? What skills/characteristics do you already have that will help you achieve them? What do you hope to gain from the degree and how do you feel it will help you achieve the career objectives that you have? (500 words)

As an aspiring entrepreneur, I believed that "my place" in the world was wherever I wanted it to be. I made my belief come true by launching my own beverage company after graduating in 2009. Despite working on a marketing budget that was less than 5% of the big corporations, I penetrated the market successfully and launched several products which became popular.

Launching and growing my business singlehandedly has given me exposure to Manufacturing, Raw Material Procurement, Packaging, Sales, Marketing and Finance. I have innovatively increased my company's market share and launched products in different States and regions, each having their own excise policies. My excellent people skills have aided my growth phenomenally, helping me strike connections with my customers and industry leaders and stalwarts. I am as comfortable "Spot Selling" my products in a pair of sandals, jeans and t-shirt every week, as I am interfacing with eminent Trade Mark attorneys such as Virendra Tuljapurkar and Pravin Anand. Now, I want to grow aggressively.

My immediate goal post MBA is to launch several new products. I also want to partner with international companies and establish symbiotic relationships where we market each other's products in areas of strong penetration. Long-term, I foresee myself as Chairman of a holding company with diversified interests in the beverages and hospitality industries.

Getting a holistic understanding of all business verticals, especially marketing and strategy and decision-making, is essential to hone my business skills. I also want a more thorough grounding in the skills of entrepreneurship — locating and networking with strategic investors, developing a more thorough business plan (so far, I have been relying heavily in intuition and past experience), and handling the financial functions more efficiently. I want a rigorous, efficient and accelerated way to realize my goals and expand my company in line with my vision. The rigorous, fast track MBA offered by Cambridge fits my professional needs perfectly.

Leadership development opportunities through relevant seminars and *Leadership in Action* will give me the opportunity to appraise myself and my skills and hone my style. The unmatched experience of learning from eminent industry specialists like Lord Dennis Stevenson and focus on Entrepreneurship through the various electives and the *Cambridge Eco System* ensures me that here I will nurture my dream of growing big. My interactions with alumni and current students (names mentioned) confirmed my belief that Cambridge is the perfect fit for me.

From my side, I promise to enrich classroom discussions with my unique experience of initiating and successfully running an FMCG company in India, an emerging economy. I can share the opportunities, challenges and bottlenecks faced in such projects, especially in the context of emerging economies and make classroom discussions more insightful and engaging. Sharing and learning will also contribute to my own growth, deepening and widening the curve of my own learning.

9. Why are you applying to the HEC MBA Program now? What is the professional objective that will guide your career choice after your MBA, and how will the HEC MBA contribute to the achievement of this objective? (500 words)

My first job with Maharashtra Knowledge Corporation Ltd., as a Network Engineer lasted roughly a year. In 2006, I switched to Verizon Data Services, where I worked until 2009. Around that time, I developed an avid interest in stocks and financial markets. I explored the possibility of a job in which I could integrate my IT expertise and interest in Finance.

This opportunity came through an opening with Fidelity in 2009, a company focused on financial markets. Despite a technical role, my excellent project management won me appreciations from both our onsite and offsite management and a promotion last year. Due to my experience of working with the client managing team in the US and developing products for various financial businesses, I have gained an in-depth understanding of the financial products and markets across the world.

Since the last four years, I have also been investing successfully in the stock markets and interacting with professionals in the Finance industry. This, coupled with the exposure that I have received through my Fidelity stint, has convinced me about making a complete switch to the financial industry. Given my current professional standing, this switch is not possible without an MBA with a specialization in Finance.

Immediately after my HEC MBA, I aspire to join an Asset Management Firm, such as UBS or BlackRock, as an Equity Research Analyst. A thorough understanding of technical aspects of the Financial Markets, coupled with the HEC MBA, will help me fit into such a role seamlessly. As I gain experience, I foresee myself becoming an eminent Portfolio Manager. With these ambitious goals, I critically need to develop strong business acumen and a detailed knowledge in Finance to embark on my new career.

The HEC MBA is an extremely attractive option, because of its well-designed, intense and evolving curriculum, which will guarantee me an opportunity to achieve my learning goals. While researching on the program, I was very excited to learn that 70% of students are career changers, just like me. I also read about the success the school has achieved in helping the students get placed in the industry of their choice and the excellent work the Career Development Center is doing in this direction. In addition to the core courses and electives, the option of specializing in Finance fits my MBA requirements perfectly. "Learning by Doing" will help me relate to and apply theories learnt in the class to real business situations.

The school's huge class diversity will be a considerable advantage for me to build a network of people with similar interests, as well as enhance my learning through sharing of vital career experiences. A strong alumni base of more than 47,000 will prove to be the gateway for creating strong networks. Lastly, the powerful brand name of HEC, consistently ranked No. 1 in Europe, will automatically open doors of opportunities for me and truly put me on the path of success for realizing my professional aspirations.

10. SOP for IIMC

I was a regular mud in the nails kind of boy. More outdoors than indoors and constantly reprimanded for playing out late and getting hurt too frequently. Scraped knees and bruised elbows were regular features of my life. Cricket and ping pong were my passions. I also played a lot of football and badminton. An introduction to sports early in life instilled discipline in me, introduced me to the importance of teamwork and taught me to stay balanced, regardless of a victory or a defeat. At home, my father's absence for long durations on account of his Marine Engineering job inculcated a sense of responsibility early in life and kept me out of mischief, synonymous with young boys.

Consistent excellence in academics and sports in school and college, coupled with strong analytical skills, led to my selection at the IT bellwether — Infosys. My business acumen and strong communication skills helped me carve out a steady growth trajectory for myself. Now, nearly 11 years of professional experience in the fast paced IT industry have provided me with rich and varied experiences and have helped me evolve as a leader. In my 6 years in the US, I have been fortunate to work amidst clients and professionals from diverse cultures like Japan, China, Philippines, UK, USA, Canada, etc., which has helped me adapt to different work cultures.

Work experience, while leveraging strengths and improving weaknesses, emphasized that now is the time to further improve my management skills, sharpen business acumen and develop 21st century leadership capability, in the best learning environment. I foresee a huge demand for technology and business savvy individuals who can manage an enterprise profitably. Undoubtedly, there is no school like personal experience, but, with time being critical, no superior methodology exists than a masterfully administered business framework.

Post MBA, I want to move into a Middle or Senior Management position in a leading IT company like Google, where I can develop strategies and integrate them with outstanding implementation. Eventually, I envisage myself as a CTO of a large corporation. The confluence of my strong technical background and a solid business foundation will help me play a vital role in strategically leveraging technology to develop winning solutions for my organization.

IIMC's reputation is almost unrivalled for transforming individuals with potential to corporate leaders. My ambition to be at IIMC comes from the conviction that nowhere else can I better acquire knowledge to emerge a complete leader.

The school's emphasis on International Business Management and Designing Effective Organizations taught through a combination of theory, case study and research papers, will provide me high intensity exposure to management. Through the International Immersion experience, I will augment my global exposure and hone my ability to collaborate with, persuade and lead multicultural teams. I look forward to contributing to group interactions and sharing my experiences of working with diverse professionals with high performing peers. With such a stimulating experience, IIMC will surely help me reach the pinnacle of success.

Goals

11. Please give a full description of your career since graduating from university. It should be written as if you were talking to someone at a social gathering, detailing your career path with the rationale behind your choices. Discuss your short and long-term career aspirations. (350 words max.)

Right after completing my under graduation, I joined the technology giant Siemens, to apply and hone my learnings of under graduation studies. I was the only one of seventy new recruits to be given a client facing role, owing to my good communication skills and strong grasp of new products. As a part of a four member sales team, I marketed contracts for electrical equipment of power plants. In this short but productive 11 month stint, I helped Siemens bag a USD 50 million contract from NTPC.

But, all along, I envisaged myself as a future, aspiring entrepreneur and wanted to work in a start-up environment that was driven by novel and niche ideas and believed in entrepreneurship to move the aspiration towards reality. I was fascinated by young and ambitious companies and joined i******, a boutique technology and litigation consulting firm with primary expertise in intellectual property and also a firm that fitted the bill in terms of the work and work environment I was looking for.

In i******, I work as a litigation and technology consultant for multiple law firms and corporations for patent litigation and intellectual property monetization. I help law firms and corporations unlock and protect the value of patents by creating leverage through a combination of deep technology expertise and practical business insights to monetize patent portfolios and profoundly improve litigation outcomes.

My distinct professional experiences have endowed me with unique skills and knowledge and also laid the foundation for my future goals. The world of Intellectual Property is stimulating, exciting and challenging. I want to get an MBA from a premiere business school like INSEAD so that I can join another young IP firm again, in a Business Development role. I want to be in a business driving role and be responsible for generating revenue for my company and do so with contextual and formal business knowledge. Acquiring and handling multiple client accounts independently and solving all arising issues in project execution will prepare me well for starting my own company in the field of Intellectual Property in about 5 to 7 years. I am open to coming back to i****** if such an opportunity exists at the time I graduate from INSEAD. In fact, I have discussed my plans with my organization and they have endorsed my decision and encouraged me to re-join them post MBA.

12. SOP for Olin

I impatiently brushed the hair off my face and stared down at the soil. I had just planted my third *neem* tree sapling. All around me, young kids were chattering excitedly, digging their tiny hands into the ground. It was the eve of Van Mahotsav, an annual Indian tree planting festival, and I had organized an activity for twenty kids from SOS Children's Villages in Pune, India. Believe me, it was no piece of cake!

We quickly scoped out a suitable spot along the river, but we hadn't bargained for how long digging the soil would actually take. The July sun beat down on us mercilessly as our shirts clung to our backs. I heartily wished I had the foresight to bring an insect repellant because my legs were proving to be a veritable feast for nasty bugs. But these obstacles were no match for our enthusiasm. By the end of the day, we had planted over fifty saplings, a small step for mankind but a big leap for us. Such were the small but everlasting joys I experienced that summer.

My friends were puzzled by my decision to spend the sacred break between graduation and a new job to go back to India and work at the orphanage. But the truth is, I didn't really see it as "working". The orphanage had been my grandmother's passion for as long as I remember. Growing up, I would frequently accompany her and as such realized early on the joy she felt in giving. Today, I continue to experience this same joy each time I participate at the Houston Food Bank, tutor young refugee kids at SEWA Houston, or raise awareness for nutrition through GE Volunteer Events.

GE's vast volunteer network was not the only reason I chose the company to kick-off my career. The prestigious Operations Management Leadership Program allowed me to rotate between Operations, Supply Chain, Manufacturing and Quality, and learn the ropes of leadership along the way.

My biggest lesson in leadership came during my second rotation. I was supervising thirty hourly-employees in the Rotor Assembly cell of the Schenectady factory. I arrived on the first day, armed with preconceived notions about the disgruntled union, having heard ugly stories from my peers. Right away, I started off on the wrong foot by attempting to establish my goals and expectations from the team. I was instantly met with frosty glares and snippy comments. The more I tried to assert myself, the more pushback I received and I was almost ready to quit after just two weeks.

Then after a particularly disappointing day, a kindly worker sat me down and provided some invaluable feedback. I realized I never once asked my employees what expectations they had of me as their boss. I was so obsessed with being taken seriously that I forgot to respect them in the process. For the last three years, they had faced a new leader every six months. No wonder they were disgruntled! It was time to right my wrongs.

I began by accepting my mistake and a desire to get to know each of them better. This only slightly mollified them. I will also take some time here to thank my good friend, Dunkin Donuts. Nothing like a box of assorted goodies and coffee to warm even some of the coldest hearts! Once I showed my interest in observing and learning the assembly process, their passion came alive. This hands-on lesson on the floor was better than any in-class training I could receive.

Soon, I began to notice opportunities for improvement. I created Macros for four of my inspectors, who spent a majority of their time on redundant Excel reports. The joy on their faces when they saw the magic made my day! Through a series of Lean Action Workouts, we designed a storage system for all tools and consumables and got new functioning toolboxes for everybody. This not only prevented loss of tools, but also reduced time wasted in searching for them. All it took was a renewed sense of teamwork, and the change in productivity was astonishing!

This summer I had an opportunity to visit the famed GE Crotonville, Jack Welch's Camp David-esque brainchild, and take a two week finance class. I was initially indifferent as I was solely associated with Power and Water Operations, but it really transformed the way I viewed GE as a whole.

Had I learned how to read an income statement in college, I could've used it to understand the "why" behind my goals in past rotations. This was also the summer GE sold Appliances and Synchrony Financial and acquired the French giant, Alstom. Emails from the CEO explained it as "focusing on the stronger industrial businesses," but that did little to satiate my curiosity. What drives GE, or any large/small sized business for that matter, to make decisions regarding its long-term viability? How do managers make decisions about a project's feasibility? I have realized an MBA is the bridge to get that basic understanding of all the disciplines that affect these managerial decisions.

The vast selection of employers that recruit from Olin makes it the perfect place to start the journey toward my short and long-term goals. I am highly attracted to the Strategy Consulting concentration. Post MBA, I want to work for a multinational, Fortune 500 company in a leadership program that will provide an opportunity to rotate between different functions of the organization such as marketing, sales, operations, and finance. This will help me understand what motivates each of them and interact with upper management. In the long-term, I want to ascend to a Senior Executive position at a consulting firm.

Olin's small class size and a central Midwest location makes it my first choice. Going to a small, private college for my undergraduate degree has made me highly appreciate one-on-one interaction with professors. I can also hope to form a lasting network of relationships when there are only 140 students. As a former international student myself, I love the diversity represented by each class. The India Club, Strategy and Consulting Association and Olin Cares will be a great way to meet people with common interests. All in all, I will keep an open mind as it, I have noticed, makes the world a much more interesting place!

13. UCLA Anderson is distinguished by three defining principles: Share Success, Think Fearlessly, Drive Change. What principles have defined your life and pre-MBA career? How do you believe that UCLA Anderson's principles, and the environment they create, will help you attain your post-MBA career goals? (750 words maximum)

"Catch, thief..."

I heard this shout one evening, while playing cricket with my friends. Seeing a boy running, chased by three men, I too ran after him and frayed him to the ground. Assuming he had stolen something valuable, I was shocked when I realized that all he had flicked were three samosas (Indian fried pastry, stuffed with potatoes). My guilt intensified as the men hit and kicked cruelly. I felt extremely helpless and desperately wanting to help the boy. I fetched my friends and swayed the mad men away.

Mukesh accompanied me home and we put him in an NGO. Funding his education, I taught him multiple subjects through school and, today, Mukesh is one of the most loyal employees at my father's printing press.

I have imbibed lessons of empathy, values, character and integrity from my parents through observance. My strong moral compass has guided me through adverse situations and helped me bear disappointments and setbacks with fortitude. My inclination to volunteer for social causes also arises from such an environment, which has contributed towards my developing genuine empathy and compassion for the less fortunate. Whether it is working with Population Health Service India (PHSI) or Bajaj's CSR initiatives, my motive for involvement has been to **make a difference**.

Calling myself a global citizen would not be inaccurate! Born to a Hindu father and an atheist mother, going to a Christian minority School, reading Gita at home and a Bible at school, wielding a cricket bat in the evening and watching Manchester United at night, attending undergraduate school in India, working in 4 different countries and speaking 5 languages—**diversity has remained at the heart of my life** since the beginning. All this has made me **sensitive towards different cultures and perspectives** and made me realize that **adaptability** is my second nature. So, I have broken cultural barriers and thrived working with people from different backgrounds and ethnicities.

For me, "Leadership **without ethics is like an anchorless boat.**" Having learnt values and morals at my father's knee, integrity is central to all my actions. Whether it was standing as Bajaj Constitution's harbinger to ensure Safety standards were met for operating staff at India's Greenfield project or supporting a Portuguese operating staff in France to avoid him becoming a scapegoat for a quality issue, I have always persevered and stuck to the right decision. I am a leader who leads from the front, the way I wish to be led.

My dynamic experiences across manufacturing and consulting have led me to conclude that I love stringent timelines, working with different teams and stakeholders, ideating for best possible business solutions and leading processes. Moving into **Strategy Consulting** is a natural extension of my professional pursuits. Post MBA, I intend to join the automotive practice of a top consulting firm, where I can feel the excitement of decision making and strategy formulating, which have direct bearings on business growth. Gradually, I would like to broaden my horizon and spread my wings to encompass the **Energy Sector**.

Upon research, I found that the resonance of Anderson's values with my own, in addition to the environment it creates for reaching my goals cannot be undermined. The **Consulting Track** will enable me with tools to complete my transition into Strategy Consulting, while the **Global Management Specialization** will provide an international perspective to all my decisions. In addition, **Professor Bill Mckelvey's** expertise in **Strategy Organizing** will hone my strategic orientation. Courses such as **Data & Decisions, Managerial Problem solving** and **Economics of Decision** will give me a thorough understanding of the best practices. The **Applied Management Research (AMR) field study program** will provide me an excellent platform to apply classroom tools to real-world challenges.

While the **Automotive Business Association** will help me forge strong industry relationships and foster interaction with the automotive experts, the **Energy Management Group** will provide me with a formal channel to understand **Energy** as a sector and ultimately facilitate my transition into it. Inside the classroom, **Professor Marvin Lieberman's** exploits in the automotive field, together with his expertise in **Competitive Strategy** and **Policy** will provide me with a solid foundation and excellent business knowledge to build upon.

With such a dynamic synergy between Anderson's principles and environment, tailormade to my aspirations of becoming an **Innovation Expert leading an Energy Vertical**, I believe that I will surely live up to the school's motto of **"Think Fearlessly & Drive change"** and complete my transformation into the change agent I wish to be.

DIVERSITY AND CONTRIBUTION

These essays are a medium for admissions teams to understand what unique perspective, background, cross cultural experiences or qualities you bring to the school and its community. What value will you add to the student body as a result of these?

Business schools want diverse classes and look to fill their classes with individuals who bring their own unique life experiences to the table, which enables everyone to benefit gainfully and make learning more enriching for the entire class. If the whole class was made up of students coming from similar personal and professional backdrops, there wouldn't be much learning happening!

Within the classroom, you can expect to learn as much from your peers as you do from the faculty and business schools try to create an environment consisting of diverse students so as to facilitate this kind of learning. This is why they ask you about how you intend to contribute to the school.

This prompt requires some deep contemplation to really reveal the elements of your profile. You might focus this essay on one particular theme or use it to highlight a couple of key factors that will enable you to contribute.

Of course, your work experience remains a central theme in your entire application and you may use this space to share any uniqueness of your professional life (only if it is not covered in another part of the application) and discuss how it will enable you to contribute. Also, look at all other aspects of your candidature like:

- *Activities you have been involved in*
- *Unique personal life experiences*
- *Social initiatives and community involvement activities*

1. How will your presence in the Tepper MBA program benefit your fellow students? How will you contribute to the school as a student and as an alumnus? (Maximum 300 words)

I completed schooling in Sharjah, undergrad in Trichy and then worked in Thailand, France and Germany. Adapting to my local environments, I have learnt to be culturally sensitive, while forming strong professional associations and friendships. Sharing my diverse experiences with my peers at Tepper, I hope to add value, while drawing learning from their distinct experiences.

I bring to the table an in-depth understanding of manufacturing processes of one of the world's largest manufacturing companies and its functions in areas like ergonomics, safety, process and logistics. Additionally, I have witnessed and solved the bottlenecks faced by a start-up plant in one of the most powerfully emerging economies in the world. My professional experiences can definitely make classroom discussions and project based activities more stimulating.

I can unite cross functional teams with my optimistic approach and inculcate camaraderie. Under my leadership, my people look at minor issues just as healthy challenges to be overcome with teamwork and opportunities to improve their competencies. I am equally efficient while coordinating with departments to streamline processes. Teamwork is a critical component of the Tepper class and towards this, I can contribute significantly. On an informal level, I would love to help my peers unwind after hectic study schedules by strumming chords or playing a melody on my guitar to some peppy rock tunes, while a friend sings along. Hopefully, I will forge some friendships along the way.

As an alumnus of Tepper, I will provide support to future Tepper students by counseling them on how to make the best of their Tepper experience. I will stay actively involved in alumni activities through Compass, class notes and affinity groups, while also helping fellow graduates in their careers. I also envision supporting Tepper's annual fund to the best of my ability.

2. What should Oxford expect from you? *Maximum 500 words.*

I have been running marathons almost as long as I have been working professionally. In a documentary film (link attached below), in which I was featured, I was called a woman who prevails through the unexpected. Being the first Indian woman to complete a 135 mile run on altitudes as high as 18,000 feet, I have been promoting running in the country and I want to continue this practice while studying at Said.

While at TCS, I continued my running and participated in organizing and running in a company organized race to raise awareness about breast cancer. Having lived in the US for 4 years, I learnt Skiing, Martial Arts, Taekwondo and Tang Soo Do (both Korean martial arts). Sports has inspired me to take up international travel outside of work, be it for the love of running or for Martial Arts. Sports has motivated me to learn Korean, a language difficult to master. Sports has taught me that what succeeds is not just intelligence or talent, but raw stamina, grit, coordination and most importantly, unflinching determination to push yourself beyond all boundaries and achieve targets. I have a thirst to constantly learn, evolve and grow, as is corroborated by my taking up new interests over the years and a quest to improve my skills by collaborating with multicultural student community of your MBA.

I am very excited to learn that the Oxford MBA takes pride in making candidates socially and environmentally aware. My participation in successful community initiatives will also help me contribute gainfully.

Beginning work at SG in March 2010, I initiated bicycling to work and, over a period of time, motivated more than 40 employees to join in. We then convinced the management to install shower stalls for us in the office and also began the trend of "Green initiatives," that is, bicycling to nearby places in and around Pune to foster environment friendliness. I am a two-time winner of the short 8 kms race for a charity event called "Fit for Life," with a prize money of INR 50,000, in addition to a hybrid bicycle. I have donated the proceeds to cancer research and to NGOs for underprivileged girls, both the times. Oxford MBA values of giving back to the community resonate with mine and I look forward to becoming an active member of the Oxford Business Networks for Environment and Social Impact.

I consider myself a future brand ambassador of the Oxford MBA, a person who will be committed to assimilate and to disseminate the values of the MBA program in all walks of life, as a current student and as an alumni.

3. How will you add value to the London Business School community? (300 words)

To the LBS classroom, I bring my unique and diverse Litigation and Technology Consulting experience. I can offer topics for broad based discussions and analysis, in context of Intellectual (IP) litigations and monetization challenges faced by law firms, corporations and universities. I can provide insights into nuances of litigation relevant across the world, right from complaint filing to the actual trial.

Working with multiple, cross functional professionals, from attorneys to subject matter experts, I have learnt how time and resources need to be optimized to meet stringent timelines. These lessons can provide rich fodder for case studies and case competitions. Having worked with diverse professionals from countries like Spain, Brazil and Romania, I can collaborate and work well with people from multicultural backgrounds, an essential component of MBA learning. Sharing and learning with peers from different backgrounds will also contribute to my own growth, deepening and widening my learning curve.

Also, as an aspiring entrepreneur (also a failed one), I believe my experiences and learnings can contribute to LBS's entrepreneurial activities. I can provide my own unique insights into different prospective ideas. While some may contribute to ideas in terms of finance or fund raising, I will share my unique experiences of being a part of a young IP startup which I have seen grow three-fold since I joined, a process-driven result that greatly excites me.

One extra-curricular activity that I'm passionate about is quizzing. Inspired by various quizzing shows, including the very popular show, *Mastermind*, on BBC, I became a quiz lover and went on to participate in and organize more than 100 quizzes, winning more than 30 of them. I anticipate starting a quizzing club at LBS and motivating my peers to this delightful and challenging activity, thus ensuring that a *quizzing culture* begins at LBS.

4. Tell us about an experience where you were significantly impacted by cultural diversity, in a positive or negative way. (300 words max.)

Living in 8 different cities and towns in India and studying in different institutions, I felt that I had experienced all the cultural diversity I possibly could. My impressions in life were formed, habits set and nothing could faze or change me.

Until I arrived in NYC! I was enthused, excited and totally ready to begin my international stint. I did not even have the wildest comprehension of the city's massive influence on me. What came to my mind when I first walked along the famed 42nd Street while exiting Port Authority was "fast and furious". This was no warm, cozy place with a predictable environment. There was an unbelievable pace to things. A determined and business-like single-minded focus which people showed to reach their destinations. Amidst this commotion, I sensed a nonchalance, as people went about their lives. Even at my new workplace, the intensity and pace of the work was far greater than I was used to. I believe this intensity was a mere extension to the essence of NYC.

Used to a slower and more relaxed pace of life, I was initially perplexed! Would I would ever fit in, let alone appreciate this new culture and lifestyle? Slowly and gradually though, I found myself becoming "a part of the crowd". I became absorbed by the city, even influenced by it.

Today I am that fast walking, determined, single-minded person that I gaped at when I first arrived. This influence extends to my workplace too. My hours of work, as compared to India, have reduced. Yet, I manage to accomplish much more, majorly because of the intensity the city and its lifestyle's influence over me. Overall, I feel like a much more focused and competent person, who is ready to take just about any future challenge, head on!

Diversity and Contribution

5. I am unique because.........of my inherent curiosity to explore the unchartered and not confine to *normal*.

As a kid, despite being right handed, I tried batting with my left hand while playing cricket and became quite good at it. Currently, I work on computer design software, which I can use with both my hands. So, I am a self-developed ambidextrous.

At 13, while other kids were reading comic books, I was pestering my father to teach me how to drive a car. While he indulged my curiosity as far as the theoretical mechanics of driving were concerned, it infuriated him no end when I fiddled with the wires, with my head under the bonnet. There were several appliances in my house that I took apart. Although I was years away from fixing things, the idle time spent tinkering with appliances was a true epiphany of my interests and talents.

Today I feel very proud to be the only person at Tata Steel managing a PLM team without a Master's degree. Due to my dual roles of PLM and Engineering, I frequently shuttle between two Tata Steel locations, spaced 350 km apart, which works out well, because I love travelling. I have travelled to 21 of the 29 Indian States and to 3 neighboring countries. I love meeting people and exploring new cultures and cuisines. I have eaten a Surströmming sandwich, slept on hard rocks, and travelled on top of the roof of a bus.

My streak to experiment, explore and simply live, not confining to boundaries, has led to interesting experiences that I look forward to sharing with my class at Emory!

6. A significant amount of the learning takes place through students sharing both inside and outside the classroom. Describe how your overall experience, both personally and professionally, will benefit your classmates.

Abu Dhabi, a hub of cultural diversity, was my home for 15 years. In the 1980s, it was in its nascent stages of development and had almost no manufacturing industries. Most material had to be imported. I observed my father's dynamic leadership style while he managed his $0.8 MM Air-Conditioning contracting business and relationships with suppliers. This was my first glimpse of business on a global platform.

By the late 1990s, the city's business landscape changed. The number of contracting firms almost doubled. The expansion created stiff competition. Without evolving business strategies, many companies, including my father's, crashed. Although a visionary, he was late to react to the changing environment. His experience taught me the importance of adapting to change in the competitive milieu.

By the end of 2010, the opportunity to grow business out of India and lead an experienced supply chain team, as a *Supply Chain Specialist*, was exciting, more so as this role was traditionally assigned to a *Supply Chain Manager*. I was a first time frontrunner, so the onus was immense. Initially, despite having a $14 million spend, there were no plans by Executive Management to grow business here. The overall vision was lacking for the region. Drawing from the learnings gleaned from my father's mistakes, I recognized that, without focusing on growing and adapting to India's changing business landscape, we risked losing out on significant market share.

Acting upon my own initiative, I developed a business plan for the Executive team, highlighting India's 7–8% GDP annual growth rate, with 40% due to increased productivity, low carbon emission rate per capita and a strong, existing

Diversity and Contribution

supplier base. Also, I highlighted that, historically, the On-Time delivery score for Indian shipments was 85% and quality score was 97.3%. Both scores were significantly higher than other low cost countries — China and Russia. The presentation hit the mark and my persistence paid off.

I was to lead the India sourcing team, create new initiatives and grow business by 20% within a year. I branded the initiative "Rediscovery of India". I endeavored to scrutinize the overall cost model and ensure that the growth provided tangible and environmental benefits. To extract the rolling demand forecast from SAP on a regular basis, I worked closely with the *Demand Management* team in order to learn the process. After studying current agreements and recommendations from the Indian sourcing team, we shortlisted three strategic suppliers for further discussion.

To facilitate learning of the business in India, I set up conference calls and virtual live meetings with the Indian sourcing team. I scheduled the calls late at night or early in the morning to accommodate the team's schedule. Soon, I flew to India for a seven day road trip to meet them and prospective suppliers. My team members included a local Supply Chain Manager with 30 years of global experience in the Energy Industry, a Sourcing Manager and a Metallurgist with 29 and 15 years of experience respectively.

I knew it would be challenging to manage such a strong and experienced team. I had to lay out the expectations. Simultaneously, I wanted to understand the issues that prevented them from growing the supplier spend in the region. Based on our discussions, I deduced that the sourcing team lacked an understanding of the SAP ERP system to extract and analyze data. The lack of this knowledge proved detrimental towards expansion. In order to maximize team performance and leverage their strengths, I expressed a need to set up a training session to help them improve their understanding of the SAP ERP system. I also set up Six Sigma training sessions to better equip them with tools to improve supply chain processes. The sessions were interactive and fruitful. They helped create teamwork and respect. We were now ready to work as a team for our meetings with suppliers.

I was not surprised to find that the suppliers' primary concern was the lack of visibility of the Cameron demand. To this, I assured them better involvement and reiterated that our regional sourcing team was fully equipped to provide them that information. The meeting were fruitful. We signed the consignment agreements, and the suppliers prepared to ramp up production to supply to global locations.

I could not have been more proud with our 2011 year-end results, as we achieved a staggering 37% increase in business from India, while maintaining high performance scores. This experience honed my ability to facilitate business partnerships. I came away with a strong belief in team projects and group environments which facilitate all members to gain superior effectiveness and team camaraderie.

My broad personal experiences of growing up in culturally diverse environments, combined with my professional experience to strengthen teams, as outlined above, will enable me to directly enrich my classmates at Duke. I will promote an environment of trust, cultural awareness, accountability and a focus on results that will strengthen team spirit. At the same time, I am aware that my class will consist of individuals with broadly different experiences and perspectives, who will enrich my learning as well and further my growth as a person.

7. What value will you add to London Business School? (300 words)

Calling myself a global citizen would not be inaccurate. Having lived all across my country, adaptability is my second nature. This helped me tremendously during numerous stints abroad for work and pleasure. With professional experiences at Bridgestone spanning 3 different countries, I am able to work and produce results irrespective of cultural barriers and can adjust to an alien environment effortlessly. Resultantly, I have gained an in-depth knowledge in the area of high volume manufacturing.

From me, students can directly leverage an understanding of the management aspects of the manufacturing industry to become more effective managers. I will also bring a truly international perspective to class discussions and social interactions.

I have an extremely positive attitude, which makes me an excellent team player. I can effortlessly unite multifunctional and cross cultural teams towards common goals. Teamwork being such an important part of the LBS curriculum, I would contribute hugely to making teams successful.

I have always striven to supplement my professional and academic experiences with extracurricular involvement. For example, I am currently volunteering for my company's CSR initiatives in neighboring villages of Chennai, in which we organize camps and drives for health and education. During under graduation, I was an active volunteer in college events and festivals which helped me in building on my team skills and coordinating abilities. My participation and leadership in extracurricular activities will undoubtedly continue after entering business school.

Lastly, I believe I have the best of both worlds — an engineering degree from a top 10 Engineering college in India and a management experience from a Fortune 500 company — a leader in its sector, with exposure to ergonomics, safety, process, purchasing and logistics. I can discuss and collaborate on a variety of topics and contribute to enriching the London Business School experience of my fellow classmates.

Diversity and Contribution

8. What personal qualities or life experiences distinguish you from other applicants? How do these qualities or experiences equip you to contribute to UNC Kenan-Flagler? (300 words)

I have supported my father's ailing transport business for two years and revived it back to life. With increase in competition, our business slowly declined and to arrest this decline, I worked on cutting out the middle men and dealing directly with our clients, i.e, the manufacturing companies using our services. I also convinced my father's fellow businessmen to pool resources and work under one umbrella, which increased our resources and strength and gradually bought in more business.

Further, I implemented a wage system in which we paid the truck drivers on a per kilometer basis, instead of monthly salaries, which bought in accountability and efficiency. Today, our business is thriving again, with a threefold increase in quarterly revenues, as a result of the innovative changes we brought in. I am proud that we have also exceeded our original targets by 20%.

Playing a pivotal role in transforming the family business has been an invaluable learning experience. I learned to gauge my audience and mold my communication to make it agreeable to them. Overall, this experience taught me to trust my instincts and not falter in trying situations.

I aim to bring to the Kenan Flagler class, skills like problem solving, innovation, and most of all, convincing and negotiating, which I extensively used during this experience. Helping turn around my father's transport business has exposed me to grass roots businesses in India, in addition to global businesses through the Deloitte stint. This gives me a unique perspective as I have seen the different challenges that are faced by these different industries.

I aim to bring forth these practical and real-world examples to classroom discussions. I also aim to join the UNC Emerging Markets Club and want to participate in discussions that will focus on doing businesses in emerging markets such as India.

9. **Cite at least one example in which your leadership impacted or changed a situation and discuss how you think IE Business School will help you refine, focus, or enhance this skill. Please limit your answer to 250 words.**

In July, there was a "Teach India" campaign run by the Times Group. This involved getting people from different backgrounds to volunteer to teach the less fortunate children. The Times Group partnered with some NGOs and placed its volunteers there.

I was one of the first few volunteers for this program and was placed at a school called Deepalaya. I taught children of the age groups varying from six to ten years. I also initiated many new extracurricular activities in the school and motivated the children to participate in them.

Once I started, I realized the acute need of educated people to volunteer for this noble cause. I got in touch with all my contacts and friends and explained the entire program to them and described the changes that they could bring about. I also shared my personal experience of the three classes I had conducted. Many of them decided to volunteer and joined the Teach India movement.

I am proud of having been able to rope in more volunteers for this movement and impacting the lives of so many children. I am now looking forward to being a part of the IE MBA, which will greatly hone my leadership skills and teach me to strategize in the best possible manner to achieve all my intended goals.

TELL US ABOUT YOURSELF

There can be several themes you can adopt for this one. You, as a unique person, have your own interests, passions, belief systems and strengths. There is really no right or wrong approach to this topic. Business schools ask you about yourself through various prompts to get to know more about you as a person. What drives you? What are your passions? And what are your priorities? What are your interests? What character traits do you possess? How do you view life?

As you answer such a question, make sure you give them an idea of your personality and an aspect which is not revealed through the other, more serious prompts and components of the application.

1. Imagine that you received an early morning call from your office telling you that due to a technical issue, the office wouldn't be open that day: how would you spend your "found time?" (250 word limit)

First, I would thank the heavens for the lucky reprieve and utilize the subsequent few hours to clean around the mess that I call home these days. Heaven forbid if my mother entered the apartment and saw the state it was in!

Next, I would call my friends and invite them over for dinner of some scrumptious Mutton Korma curry and Tandoori Roti which is Indian flat bread made traditionally in a clay oven. I do not own a clay oven, but would make do with a regular electric one. I would then go shopping for all the ingredients.

I would spend a very fulfilling day in the kitchen, stirring away my slow cooking Korma, concocting a new salad depending on the fresh ingredients available and preparing my flat bread dough. My Korma recipe is a family secret and I have frequently been told that my curries are finger licking good. In fact, those who have tasted my cooking claim that I would have made an excellent chef.

Living and working away from my family, I barely get any decent meals and rely on outsourced meal services for sustenance. And food is my passion! I love to eat and cook. Whenever time permits, I experiment with different recipes, mostly successfully, and follow a few cookery shows diligently. I cannot think of a day better spent than doing what I enjoy most—cooking!

Tell us about yourself

2. Complete two of the following four questions or statements (1000 characters per response)

   a) I am most proud of...

   b) People may be surprised to learn that I...

   c) What has your biggest challenge been and what did it help you learn about yourself?

   d) Which historical figure do you most identify with and why?

b) People may be surprised to learn that I...

....am an electronic gadget geek and my love for buying the latest gadgetry borders on OCD.

In a span of three years, I have bought 6 smartphones, 4 tablets, 2 cameras, and numerous electronic accessories. I get bored with my gadgets quickly and am forever looking for something more sophisticated and upgraded. An incident which corroborates my idiosyncratic passion for electronics is buying an electronic guitar despite not knowing how to play it. My friend wanted to buy some guitar strings and I accompanied him to this huge guitar shop in Greenville, SC. The cornucopia of electronic musical instruments mesmerized me enough to buy an electric guitar for $200. That shiny black Fender guitar beckoned me so strongly that I convinced myself that I will surely learn to play it.

I am yet to learn it after 2 years, but I am positive that I will do so sometime in the future. Till then, it sits there in my living room – an excellent conversation starter. "Oh you play the guitar?", "No, I am a shopaholic."

d) Which historical figure do you most identify with and why?

I identify with Steve Jobs. I am not an Apple lover and am totally into android, but that does not diminish my admiration for the person who built Apple with his remarkable vision and creative genius.

Steve's focus on simplicity and minimalism demonstrated his ability to correctly gauge that more features cause more confusion. I have involuntarily imbibed the quality of looking for the simplest solution from him and my experiences have strengthened my belief that clarity and focus on the objective is what matters, not how many bells and whistles you add.

Steve's tenacity and ability to learn from his failures is no secret. The sheer number of setbacks he faced in his career would have frustrated even the most stout-hearted individual. I hope to develop this impressive ability to stare down adversity boldly.

Steve's "Stay Hungry. Stay Foolish" is a motto which will inspire generations to come. It will be a long time before the world finds another iconic visionary like him.

Tell us about yourself

3. Imagine that you are at the Texas MBA Orientation for the Class of 2017. Please introduce yourself to your new classmates, and include information you feel relevant to both your personal and professional life. *Select only <u>one</u> communication method that you would like to use for your response.*

Hi!

5' 7, brown eyes, clear skin, awkward gait and wavy hair constantly falling on my forehead, I was called "Dennis the Menace" all through school. The name stuck and my childhood buddies still use it. Officially, I'm Mohit Khullar.

Punjabi by descent, Bhangra's in my blood. Once, in a German restaurant, I did the Bhangra, egged on by a friend's dare and got the whole crowd to join in. I love food, music and sports — especially Taekwondo, Football and Cricket. I am a big Sachin Tendulkar fan. Just like he always wears his left pad first, I wear my socks on my left foot first. My room at home is adorned with posters of Manchester United. That's me, personally.

Professionally, I have worked in manufacturing and consulting industries. I can speak French, Punjabi, Tamil and a bit of Spanish. Language crosses cultural barriers and this is one reason why I have thrived working with people of different ethnicities and backgrounds.

Another factor leading me to excel was my collegiate experience of leading and organizing several technical festivals and other events, while proudly maintaining academic standards at one of India's best engineering colleges. Today, once again, as I am on the threshold of my MBA experience at McCombs, I promise to uphold the school's tradition of excellence while working, learning and playing with you all. I hope there will be opportunities to dance to the Bhangra at some point, and a few of you join me to the beat!

4. Describe a defining moment in your life, and explain how it shaped you as a person.

Dreams. Passion. Determination. All of these combined and *voicehired.com* was born. Establishing this company was the defining moment of my life and as it flourishes and sustains on its own, I swell with pride to see my creation helping numerous artistes and making a tangible contribution to the society.

In college, the idea of integrating the voice-over industry originated while working on generating multimedia content for school children. We faced tremendous problems procuring the right voice for the educational CDs. I thought of starting a setup which could act as a bridge between clients and artistes. Manoj, my current VP, my wife and I started this initiative in 2011 with simply listing all voice-over artistes. Today it's a fully functional portal with project management and payment gateway integrated for empowering artistes to penetrate global markets.

Despite challenges such as total dependence on advance payment (this being an online portal), rope walking to manage expectations of artistes and the clients and delivering cost effective and quality projects in time, we have occupied our place firmly in this field. Today, we have the satisfaction of being a change agent to standardize voice-over rates in India since, currently, for the same job there is a huge standard deviation in the rates of the clients as well as the artistes.

Voicehired.com contributed largely in making me a socially responsible, competent and focused individual. I have learned the ropes of coordination, time management and strategy making hands-on very early in my career, besides getting detailed insight into the e-learning business. Recently, an elderly gentleman from a remote village called up to thank me as the portal gave him an opportunity to be self-reliant and the feeling was indescribable. This success has spurred me to establish more ventures which give me a fulfilling sense of purpose.

5. If you could change one decision you made in your life, what would it be? How would your life be different today? (250 words)

I am completely satisfied with the way my life and career have shaped up. I could not have planned it better.

That said, given an opportunity to change just one decision in my life, I would perhaps have opted for a career in Cricket. The sport is a passion for me and I excelled at it. After representing Dyal Singh College at a zonal level, I was selected amongst 30 candidates from Kurukshetra University cricket team for the Haryana state. Moreover, I was given a chance to attend a camp which could have served as a launching pad for my selection in the State and national teams. Today, I might have been playing in the national team of the country.

However, growing up, I played an integral role in my family business of farming. Seeing the lack of investment opportunities for small town businessmen like my father, instilled in me a strong desire to change the scenario. While studying commerce and finance in college, I knew that I could make a difference and realize this dream by starting an asset management company in Karnal. My experiences post under graduation strengthened my belief—and this was why I could not pursue my first love—cricket.

I am very proud of my decision and well on my way towards my goal with the MBA from Schulich. However, in moments of solitude, I often sit and wonder what my life would have been, had I pursued that path instead.

6. **Please feel free to provide a statement concerning any information you would like to add to your application that you haven't addressed elsewhere.**

I would like to use this essay to bring to light that I changed my surname from Goel to Bharat. During my college days, I became deeply interested in the great works of Swami Vivekanada and Mahatma Gandhi. These revolutionary thinkers' ideals laid the foundation for some of the most influential changes in a nation and amongst its people.

They impacted my thinking greatly and their powerful influence led me to change my last name. It was an arduous task to get it changed officially, which required many visits to government offices, invited a lot of frustration and loads of criticism from all corners.

Bharat is not my family name and certainly not the name I was born with. In fact, it is the name of my nation and transcends all barriers of caste, creed or religion. It is a choice that I made when I decided not to attend to the institution of caste in my country thereby using it as a means of boycotting the system. It explicitly and determinately means I will not believe in a system that discriminates people on the basis of anything other than their character and individual merit. Though the process of introspection and bureaucracy was difficult to navigate, the only thing that kept me going was my conviction that one day my country will overcome all barriers of discrimination and I will be a part of that change.

ACHIEVEMENTS

An achievements essay demonstrates that you have the personality and characteristics to have a definite impact on your personal or professional environment. Strong achievements essays are ones in which you affected your work environment and/or people around you in a very progressive manner and also empowered yourself along the way. You learnt something new about yourself or developed some crucial personal or professional skills which, in turn, had a lasting impact on your subsequent life. These essays will give the reader a peep into your personality, your thought process and your strengths.

As you think through your life's major achievements to decide on which one to narrate for this particular essay, think deeply about what your chosen achievement will say about you as a person. What character traits does it reveal?

Professional or non-professional examples (from your life outside of work in an extracurricular setting) can be used impressionably. If you're using a work related example, focus on how this achievement helped you progress in your career or excel in it, either tangibly or intangibly.

If you're using a personal life example, then demonstrate how the achievement prepared you for business school. For example, if you write about winning a marathon or another sports competition, you will stress on the strengths that you demonstrated, like perseverance, ability to handle difficulties and overcoming obstacles. These are the very qualities that business schools like to see, since they will prove to be a definite asset to the school.

The golden rules to follow are:
- Keep the situation in context
- Describe what you did
- The outcome of your efforts
- Your take-away from the experience

1. Pick the most significant achievement (professional or personal) you have had and elaborate on the key learning you took away from it. (300 words max.)

Receiving a merit award and a gold medal as the Most Promising Executive Trainee from an incoming batch of 600 employees from various disciplines like electrical, civil, mechanical, etc., wins hands down as my most significant accomplishment.

A stringent two-year long evaluation process, where 600 executive trainees competed in the class-room, on-job and on-field for getting the best grades, saw me putting my best foot forward. The training was comprehensive, with modules for cultural arts and spiritual enhancement and equal weightage was given to all the inputs of our performance for a balanced assessment. I stood second in my disciple (Civil) and was given a final job assignment which was, once again, up for evaluation.

The selection process for meritorious Executive Trainee started with shortlisting 50 most deserving candidates, who were interviewed by the General Manager. This group was further whittled down to 10. These 10 candidates then had to face the functional Board of Directors of NTPC, out of which two candidates were selected for the top two positions.

It was exhilarating to be chosen as the topper of my batch. My diligence, desire to succeed and single-minded focus were compensated several times over. I was justifiably proud to receive the medal from none other than the honorary Power Minister, Mr. Jyotiraditya Scindia, and was felicitated with an award by the CMD of NTPC, Mr. Arup Roy Chaudhary.

I was able to stay on top of the competition due to my ability to perform under pressure, intellectual perspicacity, and my aptitude for collaborative learning. I identified with the requirements of the training and was able to perform extraordinarily well by correlating my learning with remarkable application. I hope to perform similarly at ISB and make winning my signature style to ensure a place amongst the extremely talented pool of candidates.

2. What do you consider your most significant life achievement? (250 words)

Last December, I participated in a 100 km marathon in Ooty, Karnataka. This was my first long run. My previous marathon was only 42.19 kms. I was competing against 20 seasoned runners. Each of them had completed many long runs and I was a novice among them. Their agility and stamina intimidated me and I wondered if I would even reach the finishing line.

We all began at midnight. My only thought at that time was making the cutoff time limit of 16 hours.

Within 15 minutes, everyone swooshed past me. Each runner had their headlamps on, since it was pitch dark and we were on mountainous terrain. I kept running, keeping the closest headlamp as my beacon and attempting to close in. By the 50th km, I had overtaken 10 people. Daylight struck. The next 50 km was the way back to starting point.

I rested for 15 minutes and ate a quick meal. The roads were now open to traffic and there were no more headlamps to spot! I ran with all my might, stopping a few seconds periodically. Despite my stamina and grit getting tested to the limit, I managed to overtake 7 of the 9 runners ahead of me and finished at the third place.

This achievement was a celebration of my discipline and passion for running. My greatest accomplishment was not finishing this race but the fact that my running comrades look at me and think, "If he can, we can, too!" I see them inspired, and it feels extraordinary!

3. I'm most proud of...

.....this under-mentioned achievement, because it was through it that I cut free from the traditional mould of sticking to the safe and traditional approach that was instilled in me during my formative years (belonging to a South Indian middle class family). I learnt about the tangible benefits of taking calculated risks.

During 1st Semester exams at Xavier's, I was tackling a particularly grueling and lengthy Financial Management paper. Despite excellent preparation and research through extra reading of financial papers and journals, I could complete only half the paper in 2 of the 3 allotted hours.

Then, I spotted a bonus question carrying 30% weight. With the original paper being lengthy, attempting such bonus questions was unheard of. I decided to give it a try, albeit at the cost of the time I could use for the remaining paper, which I knew well but was unsure of completing. I initially decided to give it only 10 minutes to gauge whether I could complete it, but became confident when I asked the professor for the values for the bell distribution curve chart.

He gave me a look which was part shock, part pride and part wonder. It egged me on and I finished the question with 25 minutes left on the clock. I answered another 15-20% of the paper in the remaining time.

I got a grade A and earned accolades for being the top scorer. A calculated risk of relying on my judgment and extra reading paid off. I was congratulated by the Dean and other stalwarts—the seniors as well as the college's faculty members.

I consider this tremendous achievement to be a keystone in molding my ability to approach a problem unconventionally. It strengthened my confidence manifold and propelled me to expand my knowledge beyond the stipulated curriculum.

4. Describe an achievement of which you are most proud and explain why. (400 words max.)

My proudest achievement is winning the *Star Forerunner* award in the individual capacity and leading my 7 member team to win the *Best Team of the Year* award for FY 2013–14. These awards commemorated my team's contribution to several important projects, among which the biggest feat was helping our New York based client get favorable rulings and consequent injunctions against the Chinese telecom giant ZTE, across geographies. We seized goods and damages worth over $50 million against this infringement after I started leading the team from New York. Impressed by my leadership and the great work put in for them, the client rewarded my firm with a hefty contract renewal for services for one year, despite cost cutting plans and financial restrictions.

To begin with, I supervised the client's purchase of IP assets worth $25 million through in-depth technical and financial analysis. After this purchase, a project worth $3.5 million was assigned to us, increasing revenue by 12% since 2012.

This success led to excellent relationships with both my senior management and team members. I came to be relied upon as a dynamic leader, capable of navigating successfully through critical projects by liaising with cross-cultural and cross-functional teams.

5. What do you consider your most significant life achievement? (250 words)

I consider being awarded the Best Management Trainee Award amongst 110 new recruits in ABB during 2005–06 as my life's most significant achievement. As part of the training process, I undertook a project to analyze market opportunities of a new electrical solution for modernization of power plants.

I travelled extensively all over India, including the remotest parts of the country which were not previously covered by trainees. I visited almost all power plants and substations. I interacted with all professionals ranging from maintenance staff to senior managers and got details of old and obsolete equipments in ailing power stations. Some people were not cooperative and it took a lot of effort to gather information and documents, some of which which were more than 40 years old.

After gathering all information, I made a detailed analysis of the prospect of launching a new product in this business environment. I also researched our competition and established the timing of introduction of the product. This study gave me insights on the demographic diversity of India and different customer behaviors and industry setups.

Due of my market research, we launched our product successfully in certain territories not reached by competitors. Recognizing my capability, I was assigned as the project manager for a project to modernize power facility in a big steel plant. Usually, it takes about 4–5 years in the company to reach this position. This was a real turning point in my career path. I regard the award and the recognition as my best accomplishments.

6. What, in your opinion, have been your most important achievements? Please limit your answer to 250 words.

One of my most significant accomplishments has been getting retained by Citibank as a full time employee after just two months of training. On observing my performance as a trainee, my supervisor hired me on the bank's permanent payroll. I was one of the youngest professionals in a team of MBAs. With this experience, I learnt the different ways to deal with professionals in different hierarchies. My self-confidence increased tremendously and I gained a good insight into a multinational corporation's culture.

Motivating my mother to start painting and creating again is my second biggest accomplishment. Post my father's demise in 1999, my mother just stopped painting, which was a passion for her. She quit her job as an art teacher in a school in Muscat and we moved back to India in 2001.

I wanted her to get back to doing what she enjoyed most, which was also a medium of expression for her. I realized she needed time to heal, but I regularly discussed the various kinds of new art with her. Over the years, I motivated her to do sporadic art works and encouraged her to try new things. Over time, I became more aggressive and took her to art galleries. My patient efforts paid off and she became more enthusiastic about painting again. I am now working with her for her own venture of art works.

7. Describe a past experience where you have been strongly motivated to complete your goal.

I saw the visit of the King of Saudia Arabia as a bright opportunity to set a record of the highest sales in one day in January 2006. The King was travelling with his delegation to attend the function of the Republic Day as a guest of Honor.

I was aware that expenditure would not be an issue for the King, provided the service was flawless. I made it a point to learn about the entire delegation's dining habits and preferences prior to their check-in. I walked that extra mile to ensure that their favorite dishes were made available around the clock. I took the initiative to design and print special menu cards for the delegation, with a note welcoming them, which were placed in every room. This idea clicked, and the Room Service department succeeded in retaining all its potential customers and did not let them disseminate to other food and beverage outlets.

I also took personal charge of the operations and personally supervised the sales for all the three shifts, stretching myself for nearly 24 hrs. Finally, my decisions, understanding of the situation, and aggressive selling paid off as the Room Service department clocked the maximum sale ever in one day, breaking a nine year old record by over four folds. This record still remains unchallenged in all of the 95 ITC's hotels.

CHALLENGES

What is the reason behind business schools asking applicants about challenges? They surely do not want you to dredge up memories and recount unpleasant and difficult situations!

There are challenges associated with business school life and a management career. And admissions teams want to know if you have the tenacity and perspicacity to deal with them. The context of the challenging situation, of course, is crucial, but more important is how you handled it.

- *What actions did you take?*
- *What were your motivations behind the decisions you made?*
- *What was the result?*

Share your thoughts so as to help the admissions committees understand the rationale behind each action you took and also easily decipher the result and your key take aways from the experience. Irrespective of personal or professional challenges, aspirants who demonstrate that they've experienced adversity to reach their present standing in life will be viewed favorably by admissions team and so create power packed essays to incite empathy and interest!

1. **Describe the most courageous professional decision you have made or most courageous action you have taken at work. What did you learn from that experience? (500 words maximum)**

"Let's not think of experimenting in a client engagement," said my project lead while we were working on an engagement and were tasked to develop decision support reports, picking up business data, for an engineering and construction client.

For a small set of reports, the client wanted selling trends across multiple locations, which required extensive graphics. This was impossible with the reporting technology that was used then. Coincidently, having attended a conference on Data Visualization, I knew that it could potentially address this challenge. I researched on it further and shared my idea with my manager. I was barely one year into my stint with Deloitte and here I was making suggestions at the cost of undermining my seniors' expertise!

Since no one was well versed with it, my lead thought it would be better if we reverted to the client requesting requirement modification, citing limitations of the existing tool. However, I was confident that I could learn the tool and develop reports to meet the target, despite the stringent deadline, so I urged my manager to let me try it. He relented a little, saying that he could, perhaps, buy some time, but warned me of dire repercussions if we committed for delivery and then failed to meet the deadline.

A failed deadline would affect our image negatively. My performance ratings would dip. I would be tagged as unrealistic and irresponsible. However, I focused on the result in which we would succeed — I would walk out as a hero and bring in an innovation into Deloitte. I requested for some time to work on sample reports to prove the feasibility of my idea.

The task was not easy. I faced problems on the way, which I resolved by researching on the internet and contacting experts on the technology, through the internet.

In a week's time, after putting in a lot of hours, daily learning and developing the work, working extra over normal office hours, I was ready with a few sample reports. I showed these to my manager and further gave a presentation to the client. They were extremely impressed and agreed instantly. I was jubilant! Going further, my apprehensions were totally put to rest when we successfully used the tool. I received a handwritten letter from the client engagement partner for the remarkable contribution in the project.

Further, I worked with a manager in the service line and pioneered the sub-practice on the date-visualization within the practice, training over 100 practitioners in the process across global Deloitte offices. This experience matured me a lot in short period of time. I strongly feel that it made me a more confident leader. It taught me all about taking calculated risks and not limiting myself to conventional ways. But more than anything, this invaluable experience taught me to trust my instincts and not falter in trying situations.

Now I am a staunch supporter of innovation and encourage it heavily at work in my team and among my peers.

2. **Narrate an important/unusual incident of your life when you had to face a very demanding/challenging situation. How did you overcome the situation? What lessons did you learn from this incident? (300–500 words)**

My greatest professional challenge encompassed what I believe is the essence of leadership — Managing Change.

Being the only one from Infosys at a client location since 2006, and by virtue of the fact that I had spent a significant time there, my client team considered me one of their own. I was a part of their team lunches, weekend parties and quarterly getaways. Then, in 2008, the client's senior management decided to outsource a majority of their technical functions to Infosys, which meant that my peers from the client's IT team would be without jobs soon. This resulted in a state of ambivalence for me. On one hand, my entire client team, with whom I had spent a long time, would be going away. On the other hand, it was a big win for us in Infosys in terms of the business generated.

Knowing that my organization was responsible for their looming unemployment, I found myself in an awkward position working with the client team. In one of my sessions with a client Senior Engineer, Kathy, I asked her how she was able to identify a particular issue without even looking at the logs. With tears in her eyes, she responded, "I have been with this company for 35 years and my mother also retired from this company. So, I just know." Before I could muster the courage to say something, she recovered and continued with the session.

I was aware of their antagonism towards Infosys and the reluctance to share knowledge. A few engineers were only partially sharing information and claiming that the transition was complete. Although I knew otherwise, I empathized with their situation. I did not want to escalate this issue but, at the same time, I wanted to make sure that we received all the knowledge. Without informing the senior management, I organized one-on-one meetings with the team. I transparently shared with them that as an Infosys employee, I felt responsible for their situation, on one level, but this was a management decision. My only role in the entire situation was to seamlessly ensure a smooth transition.

Not everybody was difficult to work with. My Tech Lead, Roger, went beyond his responsibilities to help us. He not only transitioned his work very smoothly, but also offered to help with other applications. He shared his personal email ID and phone number and offered his assistance even when he was not going to be around. He showed us how a thorough professional should be.

Lastly, I whole heartedly wished them well, commiserated with their job loss and expressed interest in taking everyone out for a meal and drinks. Things went fairly smoothly after that and I received all the help from the client team. The biggest learning in this entire experience for me was that "Business is Business". One cannot allow personal emotions to come in the way of executing the overall business plan.

3. Tell us a situation when you experienced challenges in a team setting, and what you have done to help the team achieve its goals.

I was given the charge of spearheading the opening of "My Humble House" restaurant in India.

ITC Maurya, being a 27 year old hotel, has many old staff members. I observed a discord between the young and the old employees of the opening team, which was a result of insecurity amongst the old employees, and the differences in their respective view points and operational styles.

This situation was leading to delays in training, implementing SOPs, finalizing systems and standards and deciding the guest experience cycle.

I feared that this friction could result in attrition of the young associates, as enough job options were available outside in the market. I realized that the traditional system of restaurant's operations was not working.

Keeping in mind the sensitivity of the situation, I decided to implement an innovative flat structure for the restaurant setup. I removed the numerous hierarchy levels in the restaurant and chose to be supported by an Assistant Manager, who primarily overlooked the operations, and Guest Service Associates to serve the customers.

Despite all the skepticism and apprehension, I had full faith that with this style of management I could succeed in having a well-knit and motivated team with low attrition levels.

My confidence and conviction paid off as we launched the restaurant a month before the projected date, also sustaining the highest quality service standards, as revealed by the regular mystery audits and customer feedback reports.

Undisturbed communication flow, backed with zeal to perform, helped me develop an efficient team with a great sense of belongingness. Very low attrition levels were observed, too, considering that My Humble House's service team was the youngest in the hotel.

4. Describe a time in which your ethics were challenged. How did you deal with the situation and what did you learn from it?

In 2012, after I was promoted to the position of Assistant Manager of Dollar India, I came to know about a shocking management policy against employees. The production laborers were denied the standard overtime wage rate, which was double the normal rate. Instead, they had to work for extra hours on normal rates.

I looked into the matter. When I confronted the person in-charge of wages, he simply claimed that this was the norm. Next, I approached the owner of the company and requested him to make the payment policy fair. He stood firm on his ground, claiming that if he doubled the overtime rate, the company could not remain competitive enough to stand in the market.

I decided to come up with a plan that would do justice to the company and its workers. I drafted a plan of small shifts of approximately three hours for each worker on a roster system. I presented this plan to the owner and although he was reluctant initially, he agreed to give it a try. Ensuring that this special shift approach worked took an extra three hours a day for nearly a month. Finally, we arrived at a win-win situation, wherein all parties involved were happy. This was a great learning experience for me where I proved myself capable of behaving ethically and rightfully towards my organization and employees. I also saw firsthand that the productivity of satisfied employees increased tenfold which proved to be beneficial to the organization in the long run.

5. Resilience. Perseverance. Grit. Call it what you will.... Challenges can build character. Describe a challenging experience you've had. How were you tested? What did you learn? (450 words)

Confident, enthusiastic and competitive were words that described me as I eagerly anticipated college placements. I was expecting to land a job, according to my preference, at specific firms.

It was 2008, the year India was hit by massive recession. There were fewer jobs on offer and employers were conservative. Most of my peers compromised on industry or job profile. I, too, was made an offer at just one company, but declined. I held out hope for something better, but nothing materialized. I told myself not to panic as I packed my bags.

Once home, I networked extensively. The next job I applied for offered lesser remuneration than the campus offer. And I did not make the cut!

As days passed, I faced my parent's disappointment for failing to achieve what I had planned for my education. I felt pressurized and aggressively started job hunting. S***** made an offer. This time the remuneration was appalling and totally insufficient for sustenance. I had to continually supplement my earnings with borrowed money from my parents. There was much heartburn and frustration, which led to soured relationships.

I felt like a ghost of my former self and lost all the vigor and competitiveness that had landed me at one of India's top 10 colleges. After wallowing in self-pity for a while, I firmly decided to turn the tide around. Not caring about criticism any more, I decided to stick to my original plan and started job hunting. This time, I got an opportunity to work at i****** (a relatively youngish firm and the kind of company I initially wanted to work at) and grabbed it with both hands. I left S***** with aplomb, helping it win a USD 50 million contact before quitting.

It was a complete turnaround from there on. I felt reinvigorated, met some of the brightest minds, and felt competitive again. With the positive momentum, I continued improving and made international forays and worked with clients across the US. With the positivity of professional satisfaction, personal relationships improved too.

Looking back, I realize that although I initially got despondent and succumbed to pressure, when push came to shove, I realized my real priorities and stayed true to achieving my real goal.

The greatest take away from the experience was that the person you should never lose trust on when the going gets tough is *yourself*. I became ready to face the *real world*. The experience also taught me never to take anything for granted, not even family. Whether professional or personal, relationships need nurturing.

These important lessons have helped me maintain a cool outlook, while facing tough client demands or stringent timelines and are largely responsible for my current success.

STRENGTHS AND WEAKNESSES

In business school, you learn as much from your peers as you do from the faculty and the learning opportunities. Business schools know this and want to create a class full of students with their own unique strengths and weaknesses who are aware of their characteristics and want to evolve and grow. This is the reason they ask you about your strengths and weaknesses. As you figure out the best traits to discuss, think about the following:

- *Do your strengths showcase your aptitude for a successful academic and professional journey? If yes, then they are definitely worth writing about.*

- *Are your weaknesses fixable? Or, have you taken measures to overcome them? If not, then the admissions committee will wonder about your reasons for sharing them.*

1. **What are your primary strengths? What aspects of yourself would you like to strengthen and improve? What do you hope to learn during the MBA Program that will help you refine your strengths and minimize your weaknesses? (1.5 line spacing, two pages, font more than 10)**

Almost all aspects of my upbringing relate to a global perspective. I was born in Abu Dhabi, studied at the prestigious Mayo boarding school in India and completed my education in Canada and the US. To my parent's credit, I have learnt to live by the values and customs of a truly multicultural background. Growing up, I spoke three languages (English, Urdu and Bengali) and acquired a balanced exposure to the individual native languages. In school, I learnt Hindi, Arabic and French. I have seen poverty in India, rapid economic development in Abu Dhabi, diversity in Canada and prosperity in the United States. Professionally, my job requires me to work with Cameron locations and suppliers that span across four continents. A culturally diverse student body is one of UNC's most notable strengths; I can build upon this strength through my truly multicultural background, which I am very proud of and eager to share with others.

With the unique combination of breadth and depth of my professional experience, I have acquired very effective Leadership skills through diverse professional roles in the *Oil and Gas* industry. For example, I have demonstrated strong leadership in a tactical Operations environment through my role as Warehouse Manager. I learnt the various nuances of dealing with a work force from vastly different backgrounds and how to motivate each of them to perform their best. I have also worked in the Strategic Corporate environment as a Supply Chain Specialist, leading a strong technical team out of India. Working out a plan to utilize each experienced resource's strengths, outlining a vision for them and then guiding them through the entire process has been invaluable. My distinct leadership experiences will allow me to share

Strengths and Weaknesses

knowledge that will prove helpful to those students who will be taking on leadership roles to make specific changes to their organizations.

I am goal oriented, single-minded and ambitious — strengths which have helped me create a progressive career within Cameron. I have attained skills and knowledge in every position and leveraged them for subsequent roles, with greater responsibilities. Although I am ambitious, I never forget that I am a part of a team and the success of my team or organization translates to my success. To illustrate, I have built my career with one company and always considered my success to be part of the firm's success.

Juxtaposing my experience, I have limited knowledge of financial accounting and a dearth of knowledge and skills related to it. This is primarily due to my technical education and lack of managing any financials for a department. It is something which is essential for quick success in my organization and holding a key Executive position. I also feel that I can improve significantly on my Business Communication skills, which will prove very beneficial as I progress further.

I have a strong perspective on issues and sometimes, I do not give others a fair chance to air their viewpoints. This is a skill that I need to refine. I want to be a better listener and understand the opinions of others, to reach mutually agreeable solutions. What is exciting to me about the UNC MBA programme is the fact that I will be interacting with achievers from different industries and backgrounds, both face-to-face and in a virtual environment. This will allow me to observe and learn from other students how to engage in a healthy discussion without dominating the viewpoint.

Often, I tend to be impatient with those who are inexperienced. This year, I was given charge of an intern. She was from a Supply Chain background, with no formal training in any technical aspects of our business. A fresh beauty pageant winner, her attitude towards work was slightly cavalier and her questions seemed illogical and irrelevant. I found myself at the end of my patience with her, many times. I understand that I need to be more tolerant with such raw professionals and am striving to overcome this shortcoming. I want to effectively be able to mentor non-technical people to transform them into assets for the company. I am very eager to learn techniques related to guiding inexperienced resources from non-technical backgrounds. The UNC MBA will be my first exposure to professionals with expertise in different functional competencies. I am confident that these interactions and greater understanding of the different management functions will help me tremendously in this regard.

Combined with my experience, an MBA will provide me with the vital academic training in business management, crucial to my future success within Cameron. I am looking to augment my current skill set through interactions with a dynamic student body, where we can all learn from one another's experiences. I want to learn the best business practices and trends which I can utilize at Cameron to effectively lead its *Sustainable Energy Initiatives*. I look forward to building new relationships and networks within the school's community to create a mutually supportive learning environment that is unmatched in terms of learning satisfaction. I am sure that UNC will prove to be the platform where each of us can capitalize on our individual strengths and eliminate or at least curtail our weaknesses to realize our full potential.

2. To what personal characteristics do you attribute your professional success? What has prevented you from becoming more successful?

Most of my childhood was spent at our countryside farms, observing my father working tirelessly to grow seasonal crops and selling the harvest in the nearby market. Happiness meant dancing in the rain or seeing a distant aircraft in the sky. The kaleidoscope of such memories made me grounded and instilled in me the values of simplicity, honesty and unpretentiousness. I developed a frank and forthright nature due to my humble upbringing. In fact, I am able to approach problems today with clarity and directness only because of my uncluttered thought process, which I attribute to my simple upbringing.

During engineering, I was able to handle the academic rigors, not only due to my sharp, analytical mind, but also due to my ability to put in indefatigable hard work. I always considered diligence and willingness to accept responsibility to be the backbone of success.

This approach helped me particularly when I began my career with Steria and was inducted in a newly formed team for a big project. During the initial stages, the roles and responsibilities were not clearly demarcated. It vexed some of my colleagues. However, I saw it as a brilliant opportunity to gain multidimensional experiences and requested the senior project delivery manager to consider me for any area where I could contribute. Seeing my willingness, he allocated me a variety of tasks that often required me to stretch myself. In the process, I gained exceptional insights into operations of project management and learnt to interact effectively with team members. I assumed complete accountability of all the work and successfully performed tasks of increasing responsibilities.

My 18 months of intense hard work was appreciated by the senior management. I received an appreciation certificate, my first professional achievement. I was the only one in my employee band to be selected and sent to a client site—United Kingdom—for the delivery of an important project.

I take pride in being perceptive, analytical and sharp. These attributes have driven me consistently to achieve remarkable results during my academic stint and at work, too. Professionally, I have consciously enhanced my ability to apply my analytical skills without losing focus on the big picture. Such an outlook has ensured that I remain at the forefront at work. I am amongst the elite team of Card Capability Specialists, which consists of only 5 personnel out of the 600 strong support staff spread across 3 continents. We support the entire card application processing, with our capability to fix any problem arising out of the 10,000 programs within the card processing suite. My job necessitates good analytical skills, knowledge of the entire application processing of the cards and banking domain, and an ability to deliver timely results.

Juggling multi-dimensional responsibilities, I have developed the knack of taking swift decisions and conflict resolution, while managing effective stakeholder communication. Exploiting my resilience of working in critical situations, I have become adept at breaking down a problem into manageable steps, with a focus on the big picture and progressing towards its solution methodically.

My good sense of humor works as an energizer during team tasks. Witty and droll repartees often help me establish a connection with even the most reserved person. I have been at the forefront in organizing Fundays, such as team outings, picnics, etc., and I try to enhance the spirit of camaraderie in the team by personally introducing new joinees and helping them establish a comfort level with the other members.

My tendency to stretch myself to perform an entire task on my own sometimes hampers my work. In the process of taking full accountability, I sometimes misjudge others' capabilities of handling tasks. I comprehended my weakness when I was asked to lead the team for a critical project. Initially, I tackled the critical procedures myself, but while interacting with the team, I often found the team members coming up with excellent inputs and some unique solutions after brainstorming and prototyping. My trust in my team increased manifold and it helped me to drive them for successful results. This also affected my team positively and enhanced their motivation level. Since then, I make a conscious effort to pool everyone's inputs to formulate better strategies for a given task.

Another aspect which sometimes impedes my functioning is lack of experience and skill in the areas of forecasting, budgeting and managing financial aspects of the business. Had I got better financial skills and knowledge, I would have been in a better position to take complete control of project delivery and thus would have definitely gained an edge. An MBA will certainly bridge the gap between my skills and knowledge with the latest business practices and help me in leveraging my analytical skills and leadership capabilities more effectively.

3. To what personal characteristics do you attribute your professional success? What has prevented you from becoming more successful?

Passionate, Inquisitive, Driven are some of my personal characteristics that have led to my professional success. With single-minded devotion, I have seized opportunities and made conscious efforts to enhance myself professionally. I have extended myself beyond my core domain of development and contributed in various other fields. A strong believer in collaborative teamwork, I have strived to be a proactive team player in my key work areas.

I always ask myself, "Am I learning anything, becoming brighter and a more effective contributor at my workplace?" If I am learning at a slow pace, I am unhappy. Obviously, no one wants to be overwhelmed by a surplus of non-reachable learning milestones, but I have stretched myself beyond my core domain of development and made conscious efforts to contribute in various other fields like Implementation, Requirements gathering, Testing and Support to widen my learning curve and get a more holistic understanding of the core banking domain.

There has been no clear demarcation of key work areas; all work done and contributions made have been a team effort and thus the success is a result of collaborative teamwork. I feel immensely satisfied that, in the past five years, I have endeavored to take my learning and experience to the next level.

Another key strength that I want to highlight is my ability to fearlessly lead groups of motivated people in the relentless pursuit of initiating change. For example, when I joined Infosys's CSR arm, Jagruthi, in 2012, it was strapped for funds and lacked direction among volunteers, with initiatives limited to providing meals to homeless or donating books. Upon joining, I liaised with existing volunteers and conducted impromptu sessions during lunch hours or breaks to rope in more volunteers. We motivated everyone to contribute or participate and launched many new initiatives like sponsoring the education of Infosys's security guards' children and meritorious yet needy students from two government schools. Many more such initiatives followed and today we have grown our capital from INR 9,000 to INR 75,000. I got like minded people together to work cohesively and make Jagruti work like a well-oiled machine—truly living up to its motive of working for the needy social groups surrounding it.

I have one weakness that I believe I need to overcome in order to become more successful. I can sometimes react emotionally and irrationally. In 2012, I became frustrated because of lack of promotion, despite getting excellent performance ratings and high recommendations. Getting passed over by someone with lesser rating was the last straw. I angrily shot off a separation mail to my manager, expressing my frustrations. He called me for a one-on-one meeting and let me vent it out and unburden myself, assuaging my anger. He then calmly explained to me that genuine interest in my work and commitment to delivering quality output should be our key driving force. I had outshone in my career so far and should not let one missed promotion deter me. He also promised to look into the matter and motivated me to take up an extremely challenging enhancement project related to compliance from our US client. Although not fully convinced, I decided to do an impeccable job of this project, just to prove my mettle before I quit. Notwithstanding the stringent timeline and quality adherence, I completed the work in two weeks, with zero defects. Although I had felt good about my work earlier, the pride and joy I felt after completing this project, with my manager's advice resonating in my mind, was unmatched. I received recognition in the form of awards, both in individual and team capacity!

I continue working at Infosys, but this experience was a reality check and made me aware of my shortcoming. I realised that I had a myopic view of myself and my dented ego led me to write that separation mail. I have learned not to look at immediate short-term gains but just concentrate on my work and the rest will eventually fall in place. The focus of professional and personal pursuits should always be a desire for learning and excellence. Incidentally, I received my promotion this April!

4. **Give a candid description of yourself (who are you as a person), stressing the personal characteristics you feel to be your strengths and weaknesses and the main factors which have influenced your personal development, giving examples when necessary. (600 words)**

I believe in continuous action. Excelling in Sports since childhood, I participated in many competitions at interschool and college level. Cricket instilled discipline in me and introduced me to the importance teamwork. I believe that Sports teaches us several things about life and keeps us physically and mentally fit. At home, my father's absence for long durations on account of his Marine Engineering job inculcated a sense of responsibility early in life and kept me out of mischief, synonymous with young boys!

Being insightful and taking a holistic view of things are my strengths. This, combined with strong communication skills, has powered me at work. I helped Infosys win a million dollar project in 2011. Our client was working on a business transformation program with multiple vendors and assigned one of the projects to a Philippines vendor. That project was regularly missing deadlines and facing a string of issues with some deployments. During a client meeting at the US office, I proactively put forth my suggestion of assisting them with resolving issues. They agreed, and with Infosys' intervention, the deadlines were met. The client management team was so impressed with our hands-on approach and working methodology that they awarded that project, and subsequently the entire program, to us. This contract value was worth around $1.1 million and helped me win the second MVP (Most Valuable Player) award.

I am also extremely versatile, with a flair for managing resources effectively. Inducted into managing a multi-year transformation program for a US client, involving a niche technology, my program was grappling with high attrition. It was a challenge to retain knowledge. My solution was to create a Wiki site with information about the project domain, technical artifacts for niche technologies, induction plans for new members and team building sections. I utilized existing resources without straining the budget. With this measure, we were able to reduce the ramp up time of new resources from 4 weeks to 2 weeks, without a need for a separate instructor, thus leading to increased productivity. We also used the Wiki site for team activities. This Wiki site was nominated for Knowledge Management Jamboree contest, featuring a large number of projects in Infosys, and won the 1st prize in 2013.

My work has given me the opportunity to interact with professionals from different backgrounds and cultures, which has greatly broadened my knowledge and made me very adaptable. I intricately understand the working cultures of professionals and clients from different backgrounds like China, Japan, Philippines, USA, etc., and can mold my working style according to theirs.

At Infosys, I have been identified for my Leadership potential, been consistently rated among top 5% (exceptional performer category) for 4 consecutive years, from 2009 to 2013, which is extremely rare. With fast track promotions, I quickly rose the ranks and today, 40 resources report to me. Some of the Leads reporting to me are more experienced than me. However, due to my transparent management style, leading by example and being ever-present for my team, I enjoy an excellent relationship with each one of them.

I usually have set views on handling projects, based on my experience, and have to be convinced logically to accept another's perspective, a clear weakness. Further, although I pride on being open-minded, I struggle with accepting criticism. I believe that since I am details oriented, I find it difficult to admit any lapse on my part. I am making conscious efforts to be more receptive to others' ideas and criticism. Interacting and working closely with a truly multicultural student body at INSEAD can help me tremendously in becoming more amenable.

5. **Give a description of yourself, stressing the personal characteristics you feel are your strengths and weaknesses. (IIMC)**

My friends and colleagues describe me as a pleasant, hardworking and intelligent person. In my opinion, the most distinguishing aspect of my personality is my interest in varied topics. I enjoy learning about a plethora of subjects, including the Sciences, Arts and Philosophy. In my quest to explore and learn, at my workplace, too, I have made a smooth transition from being a "techie" to a professional with a natural flair for management.

My biggest strength is my ability to introspect, strive for constant improvement in myself and take feedback constructively. During my first year in OFSSL, when I failed to get the appraisal I thought I deserved, I approached my group head to discuss the same. Instead of carping about the situation, I worked constructively on the advice he gave me, and ultimately did better the next time.

My interpersonal skills are another key strength which have helped me not only get along superbly with my seniors, peers and juniors, but have also earned me tremendous respect at work. I believe in leading by example and motivating my team continuously by appreciating their efforts and being present for them. I draw inspiration from one of my clients, who was also my supervisor in 2008. I agree with him in his belief that the time one loses respect is when one demands it. He admonished in private but praised in public. I have tried to emulate his people skills in both my personal as well as my professional life.

I consciously endeavor to seek newer challenges and to avoid complacency from setting in. After the first five years in Services Division in my organization, I shifted to the Product's Division to acquire in-depth knowledge about my company's flagship product. By shifting base, although I had to start afresh, I reveled in absorbing all I could about our banking solution product—Flexcube, which has been billed as a top selling banking solution by International Banking System, UK. Four years into that decision, I find myself better placed at my work place — with a unique distinction of having worked in different divisions and with significant domain expertise and a wider view of company operations.

One trait, which I consider a weakness and am trying to improve, is my impatience with people who I feel do not share the same drive as I do. I attempt things passionately and take ownership of whatever I do — both in my personal as well as my professional life. This sometimes makes me overtly critical of people who appear to be less driven. However, I realize that it is not right for me to be excessively judgmental especially since I have been proven wrong on occasions by such apparently laidback people and am trying to overcome this shortcoming.

5. As a Fisher College MBA student, you get the best of both worlds: the up-close and personal feel of a small program, combined with the resources and opportunities offered by a major research university. As an individual participant, you will play a key role in shaping our culture. Consequently, we would like to learn more about who you are and the unique characteristics you will contribute to the Fisher College community. Provide an honest description of yourself outside your professional context, stressing the personal characteristics you believe to be your strengths and weaknesses, along with the factors that have most influenced your development to date.

I am immensely proud of the fact that I have the determination and courage to face any curveball that life may throw at me. I am confident that my will power to surmount difficulties will help me take long strides in this adventure of life. I belong to the North-eastern part of India. This region is not a very well developed one, with its economy often spiralling downward due to ethnic friction, violence and insurgency. At school, lack of infrastructure made my job of competing with my counterparts at national level that much harder. But I did not give up. For my exams, I had to travel long distances and stay with relatives, but I did not lose heart and put my heart and soul in my studies. My hard work and determination was more than compensated when I found myself among the "top 50" North-eastern students in higher secondary exams and received a scholarship for pursuing college education.

Despite coming from a humble background with modest means, I consider myself rich in personal qualities and abilities. My parents ensured that I never lacked in opportunities which built my character and instilled a very high standard of moral values and integrity.

My government scholarship was a boon to me as it hugely reduced my college expenses and allowed me to participate in college events. I had not got much exposure

Strengths and Weaknesses

of participating in extracurricular activities at school level and I took this opportunity to participate and coordinate college festival events. Often, I had to travel to metro cities to get sponsorships for organizing events and I used my own money for my expenses. I also participated wholeheartedly in NSS at college and did my bit of shouldering social responsibility by helping slum dwellers through medical camps and providing school books and accessories.

To me, commitment and integrity form the core of a person. A strong moral compass guides a person through challenges more effectively. My family, friends and relatives find in me a strong support pillar, as well as an anchor in times of needs and I have often helped them in their difficult times. At work, too, my endeavor has always been to ensure smooth production at the factory, and finding ways to enhance it. I do not hesitate to go beyond my scope of work to ensure meeting the target. For instance, I successfully coordinated with the maintenance unit to manage production delay during breakdowns of machinery and ensured periodic shutdown for preventive maintenance, thereby reducing the effective delay of production by 348 hours in the year 2012-13.

Cleanliness is next to Godliness and I like to have my surroundings scrupulously clean and neat. I genuinely believe this reflects my personality too. I adhere to very high standards of cleanliness at home and at work. On site, I ensure that all spillage is effectively dispatched to raw material yard, ensuring no metal scraps and flammable material are found in the work area.

Analyzing my weaknesses, I feel that I am not very assertive. Since I believe that every person needs to have his or her say, I often end up not being able to put my foot down when required. In the process, while considering everyone's opinion, I often get less time in planning my work correctly. However, I am confident that I can improve on this weakness and focus on the target more forcefully. Secondly, an eye for detail leads to adding stress when I have to achieve a target. Whether it is putting up a painting at home or working in a project at work, my endeavor is to get a "perfect" outcome. In the process, I end up spending more time than required. I need to work on better planning and adopt a more rational outlook towards achievement of targets to create that fine balance between work and effective and timely outcome.

My qualities have been the cornerstone of my personal growth and I consciously imbibe values from personal experiences to augment it further. I cannot imagine gaining my professional success in the absence of my personal strengths. My characteristics have helped me flourish as a person, as well as at work, and my confidence in my abilities has only increased with time.

Mingling with the diverse fraternity of Fisher MBA will further widen the horizons of my cultural and social mindset, making me more adaptable. I hope to step out of Fisher as an accomplished, broadminded and talented individual—a true global citizen in every respect.

LEADERSHIP AND TEAM SKILLS

These essays are mostly behavioral, asked for the simple reason that your past behavior is a fairly good indicator of your future performance as well. Business schools are looking to groom future business leaders and they want students who have the potential to make an impact.

Team based essays are a means to evaluate if you will be able collaborate effectively with your classmates at B-Schools and later with the teams you work with, post MBA. Many times, as demonstrated through the sample essays, the two go hand in hand.

Mostly, when answering such questions, ask yourself:

- *When did you build a team that faced challenges and excelled?*
- *What were the expectations?*
- *What impact did your team have and how did it achieve and surpass expectations?*

1. Describe a workplace situation where you had a responsibility for managing people. Reflect on what you learned.

As a Business Unit Leader, my daily job involves managing teams of operators and technicians and coordinating with professionals from other departments. However, there is one special situation I want to cite, where I learnt tremendously.

During the commissioning phase of the machines in my shop, we witnessed numerous unforeseen delays due to the building construction not being completed and some machine parts blocked at customs. My team members had been trained on these machines in France and Germany and were eager to begin work in India.

The delays affected their enthusiasm levels and left me worried about them losing out on their expertise. Each time the commissioning audits were rescheduled, I had to update a lot of documents, coach my team to make sure that they had not forgotten the important aspects regarding safety and quality, and coordinate with other teams to ensure that all supporting documents for machines were in place.

However, I utilized this period to spend individual time with each team member, organize regular refresher trainings for them and also delegated a few of my responsibilities to further develop their skills and competencies. We strived hard to maintain our motivation levels as a group, share our grievances and keep an open communication channel so that when the time came to begin work, we would be ready! My proactive approach and complete involvement with my team helped me ward off despondency. I pushed through this period diligently and the third time, after 4 months, the commissioning finally happened and I received immense appreciation for my contribution from the management.

The most important lesson I learnt was that a leader who adopts a transparent leadership style, keeps his team's goals above all else and builds people, resulting in committed work groups, eventually succeeds in any undertaking.

2. **Leadership and ethics are inevitably intertwined in the business world. Describe a situation in which you have dealt with these issues and how they have influenced you. (250 words)**

When I joined Sungard, I became part of a team consisting of three programers working in collaboration with 8 senior US employees based out of North Carolina, US. I showcased my leadership by delivering a critical project, without assistance from the US staff, in 2010.

Resultantly, I was promoted to Team Leader, ahead of my teammates who had more experience and had joined Sungard five years earlier. That time I did not pay much attention to this out of turn promotion, but knew that Sungard follows a fairly non-hierarchical and flat management structure. Everyone is involved in programing and product architecture, so promotions are rare.

However, both my teammates also wanted a promotion and were contemplating a job change if it did not happen. I sat down with them and discussed their work profile individually. I frankly told them that I wanted their growth, but would recommend them only if I had sound reasons.

Then, I got them both involved in training for a new technology. Using this technology, one of them developed a fantastic tool for management reporting. During the annual performance appraisal process, I recommended her for the next level and clearly notified the other teammate about his areas of improvement.

With this experience, I learnt firsthand how difficult decisions need to be taken in a business environment, but transparent and open leadership leads to unity and productivity in the team. Both my teammates are happy at Sungard and I also saved our critical project from attrition.

3. Tell us about your most meaningful leadership experience and what role you played. What did you learn about your own individual strengths and weaknesses through this experience? (500 word limit encouraged)

December 2011, during a regular Skype call with my father, he shared that he was contemplating closing his 25 year old transport business. Ten years ago, the industry had undergone a massive metamorphosis. With easy loans, competition became rife, leading to slow deterioration.

I didn't want him to give up on this business—his pride and joy since my childhood. I motivated him to fight and got intrinsically involved with him. After analyzing key pain areas, we broke the problem into three main targets: Constant stream of items to transport for stable revenues, establish and maintain competitive wages to counteract competition, and retain better skilled staff. I concentrated on the stable revenues to survive. I proposed cutting the middlemen by dealing directly with manufacturing companies rather than through contractors.

There were only a few companies which dealt directly with truck owners. Most had strict standards. After meeting many and networking, coordinating, negotiating, we struck deals with two—one in Rajasthan and one in Sriperumbudur, Tamil Nadu—through my network (peers from IIT working in the area), to use our trucks for to and fro freight. Both companies mandated a minimum of 15 and 30 trucks respectively. We had only 5, so I convinced my father's fellow transport businessmen to club trucks and work together. With more trucks and consistent services, we could govern the terms and transport charges without getting affected by the competition.

To manage staff properly, I proposed implementing a wage system in which we would pay the truck staff per kilometer over the existing per month pay-system. This ensured that all staff were continually motivated to complete their trips in a timely manner and eliminated slackness, leading to a win-win situation for both the employees and the employers. Despite being looked upon with uncertainty in the beginning, this formula is now a super hit, with more truck owners outside our umbrella adopting it. Things started improving and we have achieved targets in the last six months.

Playing a pivotal role in transforming the family business was invaluable. I extensively used skills like problem solving, motivational skills, innovation, quantitative skills and most of all, people skills, all essential to become a good leader. This situation also provided me a unique experience of collaborative teamwork—I had to convince many individual stakeholders (aged 50+) to work cohesively for common benefits. It was challenging to break through mental blocks to alter traditional business practices.

However, I also got introduced to a personal growth area and a chance to work on it. I realized that I needed to gauge my audience and mold my communication to make it more agreeable to them. Dealing with seasoned transport businessmen, I initially got all my suggestions rejected by first ideating and then seeking opinions. I gradually changed my approach, involving everyone in the brainstorming so as to gradually arrive at the most logical conclusion—which resulted in consensus. The ideas became ours rather than mine.

Overall, this invaluable experience taught me to trust my instincts and not to falter in trying situations.

4. **Leadership requires an ability to collaborate with and motivate others. Describe a professional experience that required you to influence people. What did this experience teach you about working with others, and how will it make you a better leader? (450 words)**

In 2013, while assisting a core team of 8 members and 2 project managers for a project, I was utilizing my domain expertise to manage escalated and important issues. This critical project generated about 10% of the company's total revenue.

Three months later, both the Project Managers quit and needed to be replaced immediately. After a rigorous selection process, in which past performance, rating and project knowledge were assessed, I was chosen to lead this project. I was now in-charge of the Indian team and interacting directly with the client for deliverables. Soon, I relocated to the New York office at the client's request, to streamline the process.

Initially, the Client Management channeled their queries through the Account Manager, despite I being present. I took time to understand the core work, thought process and requirements of people at different rungs and especially the expectations of the senior management. Over the next few months, I ensured that I efficiently discussed the key issues and molded my communication according to the person I was interacting with. I handled the minutest of details and kept all the stakeholders abreast of developments.

The I******* management, too, was scrutinizing my Decision Making and Client Handling despite being confident about my skills. My peers, who were now directly reporting to me, were reluctant to adapt to the change in leadership. I needed to act quickly. With methodological planning, I interacted with each member regarding deliverables, over daily scheduled calls. This helped me to understand their personalities and their respective strengths and weakness and allocate future assignments accordingly. Also, I discussed their work products individually, and took a keen interest in understanding their viewpoints. I pitched in fresh ideas and new lines of thoughts. Gradually, over a period of time, I

Leadership and Team Skills

gained my team's trust and arrested the threat of attrition too. With the team on my side, I gained my management's trust and soon, I was given independent control and became the go-to person for this project. Its successful execution led us to win an year's extension, despite the client facing financial constraints.

My biggest takeaway from this transitory experience was that successful project execution requires successful team building. Working in NY and managing teams based out of India, I received a truly global exposure of dealing with diverse functional and technical (IP Litigation) professionals. To quote the client, "We cannot believe that you were the last member on board" spoke volumes of my leadership potential. These latent skills, when honed further through the Kellogg MBA, will put me at a distinct advantage in the future too.

For this project, my team won the best team award and I won the Best Senior Associate for FY 2013–14.

Use education, not to refine your life, but to enlighten your soul!

Mansie Dewan